THE DARK SIDE OF THE
SUPERNATURAL

BRYNNE LARSON

DESTINY IMAGE® PUBLISHERS, INC.
P.O. Box 310, Shippensburg, PA 17257-0310
"Promoting Inspired Lives."

This book and all other Destiny Image and Destiny Image Fiction books are available at Christian bookstores and distributors worldwide.

Cover design by: Eileen Rockwell

For more information on foreign distributors, call 717-532-3040.

Or reach us on the Internet: www.destinyimage.com

ISBN 13 TP: 978-0-7684-0708-2

ISBN 13 eBook: 978-0-7684-0709-9

For Worldwide Distribution, Printed in the U.S.A.

1 2 3 4 5 6 7 8 9 10 11 / 18 17 16 15

I would like to dedicate this book to my family:

Dad, Mom, Brooke, Brielle and Mimi.

There are two equal and opposite errors into which our race can fall about the devils. One is to disbelieve in their existence. The other is to believe, and to feel an excessive and unhealthy interest in them. They themselves are equally pleased by both errors, and hail a materialist or magician with the same delight.

—from the Preface to
The Screwtape Letters, C.S. Lewis

Acknowledgments

This book wouldn't have been possible without my father and mother. Also, I would like to give a big thank-you to Destiny Image Publishers for giving me the chance to share my story as a first-time author. It was an honor to work with all of you.

Contents

Foreword

By Tess and Savannah Scherkenback

Today's millennial generation lacks an authentically biblical understanding of the consequences that befall those who dabble in the occult. The result of not having healthy spiritual boundaries has been detrimental to many, culminating in shattered lives and lost souls. As the eldest daughter of the world's foremost exorcist, Rev. Bob Larson, Brynne Larson has witnessed first-hand the treacherous snares of the devil. Her mission in this book is to reveal the evil strongholds present in pop culture and to educate youth to be wary of the paranormal. This book also provides an understanding of spiritual warfare and the hidden dangers of the dark side of the supernatural.

As two of Brynne Larson's closest friends and companions, with a mutual interest in spiritual warfare, we have battled demonic forces alongside Brynne. In all of our experiences together we have recognized that the commitment and compassion demonstrated by Brynne is extraordinary for a young woman. Her faith has impacted thousands of lives and inspired young people around the world to take up the cause of spiritual freedom. As a powerful warrior for the Lord, Brynne takes a stand for her generation by constantly battling for the truths of God's kingdom.

Tess and Savannah Scherkenback, also known with Brynne as the internationally recognized "Teenage Exorcists."

Introduction

A cold chill came over the room, as if an evil presence had arrived.

Across from me sat Allie, a sweet eighteen-year-old girl from Indiana, who had been crying a few minutes ago. Now she sat glaring, her eyes full of hate. A deep, angry voice growled from her throat, "You can't have her, she's mine." Sitting at my side, my two best friends Tess and Savannah exchanged troubled glances. What had started out as a simple prayer session with Allie had suddenly taken a more sinister turn. We realized that there was more going on than simple boyfriend troubles.

Thankfully, Tess, Savannah, and I had run into this type of thing before. We were determined to find out who the voice belonged to and what it was doing inside of Allie. We asked some questions and discovered that a year earlier, Allie had gone to a witch doctor to put a curse on her cheating boyfriend. It seemed at the time that the curse had worked, because just a couple of days after, Allie's

ex-boyfriend broke up with the girl with whom he had be-
trayed Allie's trust. Allie had thought that everything would
go back to normal, but (no surprise to us), it had not.

Allie had dabbled with the supernatural. She had gone
outside of the natural world to try to fix her problem. But
with that kind of experimentation, there is always a cost.
Ever since she went to the witch doctor, Allie had been
tormented by malevolent thoughts. She suffered vicious
nightmares, and her friends noticed that her behavior had
changed drastically. She had gone to psychics, had her
palm read, and tried using an Ouija Board, longing for
some relief, but things only got worse. Now she was struggling with depression and thoughts of suicide.

Desperate, she came to us in a last-ditch effort to
get help from the personal hell that she had landed in.
Tess, Savannah, and I have a special skill set certainly not
normally associated with teenagers. We know how to cast
out demons. In fact, we have trained since the age of sixteen in the spiritual art of fighting the forces of darkness.
When I say casting out demons, I don't mean that we do
Hollywood-esque horror-movie-style exorcisms with spin-
ning heads and levitating bodies. I'm talking about down-
in-the-trenches spiritual warfare, facing real demons who
are in real people.

The three of us have looked into the face of true evil.
We've battled Satan and his minions, and we've learned a

thing or two about the dark side of the real supernatural world out there.

As Allie's story developed, it became clear what Satan's plan was. When she had gone to that witch doctor to put a curse on her ex, she had unknowingly opened up a spiritual door. There is a real supernatural world—we can't see it, but it's real. The supernatural realm is a world of angels and demons, God and Satan. Once someone decides to delve into it and opens a door into that world, they find that the door is extraordinarily hard to close. And, worst of all, it can allow demons to come into the person's life.

Allie had opened up that door by seeking a solution from the occult side of the supernatural realm. She didn't realize that she had gone to Satan for help. Just because Allie didn't realize her error did not mean that she got a free pass; she suffered serious repercussions from her actions. Unintentionally, she had allowed Satan into her life, and he was tormenting her. That's one of Satan's biggest weapons: a lack of knowledge. He counts on people mistakenly stumbling to him for help then falling into his seemingly benign spiritual traps, all because they "didn't know." The Old Testament prophet Hosea proclaimed, "My people are destroyed for lack of knowledge. Because you have rejected knowledge, I also will reject you...Because you have forgotten the law of your God, I also will forget your children" (Hosea 4:6). God doesn't allow us to simply do whatever we want just because we don't "know" that it's wrong. He has made his precepts clear, and we don't have an excuse for ignorance when it comes to spiritual matters. Playing around with the supernatural is no game or laughing matter. It's serious and can have lifelong consequences.

People like Allie are the reason I do what I do. In order to bring spiritual healing and freedom, I have learned about the supernatural, about angels and demons, and how to cast out demons. I have learned that when you sin against God by going to a witch doctor, hating or vengefully injuring another person, or dabbling in the occult, it opens a spiritual door to the supernatural side and allows all kinds of unwanted junk into your life. The best way to prevent that from happening is to educate yourself about the realities of the supernatural world. You need to learn how easy it is to fall prey to one of Satan's traps.

As we worked with Allie, she began to understand just what her actions had actually wrought. It took a while, but we were able to discover how the demons had gotten into her, then we broke the curses that she had inadvertently put on herself. This time, we broke the curse of witchcraft, because Allie had dabbled in sorcery. We also broke the curse of unforgiveness toward her boyfriend.

When we tried to break those curses all hell broke loose. The witchcraft turned out to be the demonic stronghold. The chief demon, called Witchcraft, wasn't going to sit idly by while his stronghold was broken. Screaming and thrashing about, the demons in Allie tried to keep her from breaking the curse. It was a long fight and it took hours, but finally the demons surrendered. The curse of witchcraft was broken on Allie's life. Since that time, she has grown stronger in the Lord and avoided every kind of occult activity.

People like Allie don't usually decide on a whim to visit a witch doctor to cast a potent spell. There is hardly ever an isolated supernatural incident in a person's life. People usually develop an interest or fascination with the supernatural, and this curiosity is both encouraged and cultivated by the times we live in. There is a strong pull to the supernatural; it represents seemingly endless possibilities, power, and an entrée to the vast unknown. The true cost of such explorations is not always seen. As darker supernatural ideas become more "mainstream," people like Tess, Savannah, and me are becoming more concerned.

If we are not for God, then we are against Him (see Matthew 12:30). Satan is looking to entice people away from God and His goodness. He wants to lure them away with the promise of something supernatural. But his version of supernaturalism is only a dark shadow of what God created the supernatural world to be.

We are all on one side or the other; there is no in-between when it comes to spiritual matters. A battle is underway, a fight for the hearts and minds of humanity. The battle between good and evil, heaven and hell, God and Satan, has been raging ever since Creation. This battle is not one of fairy tales or fanciful imagination, but a real battle, with casualties on both sides.

And that's why I do what I do. It's why I keep training to learn how to fight spiritual warfare. Playing around with the supernatural is like playing with fire, and those of us who do this work can help the victims who have gotten too close to its bright flame. The paranormal, occult world is real, the supernatural war is real, and the misery and pain are real. The good news is that God is greater than anything, and His healing and freedom are real, too.

I invite you to catch a glimpse of my world, a world of good vs. evil, epic spiritual battles, and a real God and a real Satan. Turn the following pages to explore with me. Let's get rid of our whitewashed misconceptions as we unmask the dark side.

CHAPTER 1

The Demon That Opened the Door

None of us does this kind of work alone. I'm part of a team. Tess and Savannah are my best friends. They are also sisters, although they are as different as night and day, and the three of us work very well together, balancing each other out. They love classic movies and singing, while I can barely screech out a Happy Birthday song and prefer reading. We met at my local martial arts *dojo*, where the three of us were training for our black belts in tae kwon do. We became friends, and one day I invited them to witness what my family has been doing for more than thirty years.

My father, the Reverend Bob Larson, has been in the public eye for decades. I've traveled with dad all over the world, from China and Africa to Australia and England. I always sat in the front row as I watched Dad work with people who were struggling with demons. I grew up seeing him cast out demons and from a very early age I knew that there was a spiritual realm we couldn't see, but it was nevertheless very real.

Still, while I thought that doing exorcisms and deliverance was really cool, I didn't see how it applied to me. I thought, "Sure, this stuff is real and amazing, but hey, I'm just a kid, why should I worry about all of that?" That outlook drastically changed on my sixteenth birthday.

You see, before there was Allie, there was Katie. My sweet sixteen birthday started off in a pretty normal way. We had cake, presents, games, and swimming—just the average teenage birthday party. One of my best friends, Katie, who had moved a couple states away, flew in to attend my party. We've been best friends for as long as I can remember. We grew up together, and she had become a godly young woman. But somehow in the year that we had been apart, she'd changed. As we chatted late that night, I found out that that she had turned her back on God and had gotten involved with the wrong crowd. As a result, she had done some pretty bad things. I prayed with her and led her back to God, and she repented and recommitted her life to Him.

Satan didn't like that, and immediately Katie started acting really strange. Because of the things she had done and the doors she had opened, the devil had been given a right to come into her life. Throughout the next day,

Katie was not the Katie that I knew. She was vague, distant, and uncomprehending. Her eyes had a glassy look, and I could barely talk with her. She complained about a killer headache. There was something dark going on. You could sense the evil and spiritual turmoil. Tess and I decided to pray with her, and that's when it—the demon—spoke to us. As we sat quietly praying with her, she looked up at me, and I didn't see Katie in her eyes. *I saw evil.* And then it whispered through her, "You can't have her, she belongs to me." Tess and I were startled—a demon in my best friend was not what we were expecting.

I quickly called Dad on my cell (he was ministering in another city), and he walked us through how to cast out the demon inside Katie. She got back on a plane that day and headed home. Providentially, my dad happened to be in the very city where Katie and her family lived. He met with them immediately and proceeded to clean up the entire family spiritually. As it turned out, they had been suffering from a generational curse that had affected them and their ancestors for hundreds of years.

Freedom came to Katie and her family, and now she is planning to go to China as a missionary. Meanwhile, Tess and I developed a plan. We now saw with stunning clarity how applicable deliverance is in everyone's life. My best friend had a demon. Quite likely others that I knew were suffering in the same way, and I hadn't noticed it before. I realized that I would be running into situations like this all of my life, and that I had a choice: I could either learn all that I could about spiritual warfare, or I could ignore what had happened with Katie and go on with my life. For me, the decision was pretty clear, and Tess and Savannah shared my inclination. So we asked someone experienced in deliverance if he would start training us on how to do exorcisms.

The Teenage Exorcists

He was reluctant at first. We were, after all, only teenagers. And exorcisms can be dangerous. But we persisted and eventually he agreed to start training us. For the next year, we met every week and soaked up all that we could on world religions, the occult, the supernatural, curses, and demons. We trained hard and committed ourselves to learning all that we could. If we came across another demon, we would be ready. Fortunately, we had a great teacher.

The man who taught us everything we know is my dad, Bob Larson, pastor, author, TV and radio host who has cast out thousands of demons during more than three decades of ministry. He has become one of the world's foremost experts on the occult, supernatural sphere. He has poured hours of one-on-one training into us. As far back as I can remember, Dad has always been in the public eye, with reporters and journalists contacting him for information about what he does and the evil that pervades our society today. Now, my father, who has spent more time learning and teaching spiritual warfare than perhaps anyone alive, was our very own, personal instructor. It doesn't get any better than that and we relished every moment he spent with us.

One day, my father was talking to a reporter from *Fabulous Magazine* (a huge online magazine in London, England), and he was asked who else did exorcisms. "Well" Dad said, "My daughter and her friends do!" Of course the journalist was shocked. How could three teenage girls be casting out demons? He asked to talk with us and to write a story for *Fabulous Magazine*. We agreed and were happy to share with the reporter about our training and what God was doing in our lives.

When the story came out, it made waves. News website after news website picked up the story, and before we knew it, we were an internet sensation. Journalists and reporters contacted us from all over the world. I was shocked at the reaction. When I googled my name, I got pages and pages of articles, blogs, photos, and videos of myself, whereas before I would have gotten nothing. I was completely unprepared for the interest that had been generated. I would never have imagined how fascinated the world would be by what we do. We were teenagers, we were female, and we were exorcists. That was a lot more than some could handle, especially some very unkind Christians.

Then our world made another lurch. World-famous journalist and television personality Anderson Cooper contacted us. He had just launched a new daytime talk show and wanted to feature us on nationwide TV before millions of people! This invitation proved to be a defining moment in my life, a moment when I had to face a make-or-break decision that would forever alter my life.

Anderson wanted the three of us girls and my dad to come on the show to talk about what we do. The production company flew us up to New York and put us up in a nice hotel, where we had several celebrity sightings. They had a hair and make-up crew waiting for us when we got to the studio. We were over the moon; things couldn't get any cooler than being in New York, about to go on the Anderson show and having our hair and make-up done by professionals. However, the stars in our eyes quickly dimmed when we got onstage.

We walked out in front of a live audience and made our way up to the couches. Right before Anderson came out, another group of people joined us onstage. We didn't know who they were, but we shortly found out, as the show developed into an attack piece. We were grossly misrepresented and ridiculed. We were told that instead of helping people with real problems we should go volunteer at a dog shelter or something. We were not given any time to talk except to answer a few questions that were designed to put a negative spin on the interview. Then we were attacked by a strange no-name preacher who got up and started acting like a lunatic. The audience was even cued to start applauding whenever something nasty was said about us.

When the director finally said "Cut!" and we walked off the stage in a daze, we didn't know quite what to make of what had just happened. Of course we knew that people would have questions, and we knew that not everyone would believe what we said. But we hadn't expected the mockery and questioning of our brains, faith, and faculties. We hadn't expected the low blows and cynicism. We were told to stop what we were doing, to not challenge the status quo by doing something bold for Christ. Anderson Cooper basically told us to play nice, and to go back to whatever crazy hole we had crawled out of because we were fakes and frauds. All of this happened, of course, on national television.

Backstage, the producer of the show apologized, saying she had no clue what was going to happen. We were more than a little stunned. This was the first real hit, and it hurt. We packed up and headed home.

On the plane we all had some serious thinking to do. We were taking a controversial and uncomfortable stand, and part of me wanted to stop. All of my friends would see this report on TV. Maybe we should do something less controversial. But another part of me wanted to keep going. There are so many misconceptions about spiritual warfare, and for some reason, people listen to us. Anderson had called us fakes and frauds, but I knew better. I knew that this was something God wanted me to do. I knew in my gut that I had to keep going, to keep training. It wasn't the most popular choice, and I knew that I would lose friends and be mocked, but if God was calling me to do it, how could I say no? How could I turn my back on all the people who need help? How could I ignore God's calling just because of a few critics?

One thing that I have learned already is that if I'm not facing opposition, if the devil is not trying to stop me, then I must be doing something wrong. We agreed together on that plane that we would be stronger, train harder, and ignore the voices of critics who would try to tear us down. Even though Anderson Cooper's show was a difficult situation, remarkable good came out of it. Looking back, I wouldn't change a thing. Yes, we were challenged; it was ugly and mean, but I came out stronger than ever. I became more determined to share the truth of what God can do through an ordinary young woman like me.

Even though we didn't see it right away, great things came out of the actual show, too. Afterwards, we had been asked to share our thoughts on a backstage cam. Through those four uninterrupted minutes, we were able to tell the viewers the things that we weren't able to say on the show. We shared our hearts and defended ourselves to tens of thousands of people. And, more importantly, people came to us to get help specifically because they had seen us on

Anderson's show. Being able to help even one person out of the misery of years of spiritual oppression is worth all of the sarcastic comments in the world.

Back home, as we sat down to watch the show, which had been taped, some of my friends showed up at the house unexpectedly. They watched the show with us, and then they got up and left without a word. I was surprised and a little hurt. We had just taken a beating on national television, and I expected my Christian friends to support me. There was no support...and that's OK. It took a while to come to this point, but the truth is, I don't need the world's approval, I need only God's. That's not to say that I'm some sort of iron wall. When people are nasty and say awful things about me and to me, it hurts. When I lose friends because they don't like what I do, it hurts; but I believe that is a very small price to pay for the freedom of thousands of people. If what I do is easy, then everyone would want to do it.

Anderson Cooper was the first big bump in the road, but he helped Tess, Savannah, and I make our decision. We were in it for the long haul. We were now officially the Teenage Exorcists!

None of us magically started at the point of being able to face demons fearlessly. It took hours of hard work and studying and practice. As our public profile grew, in large part due to media interest (*Good Morning America, Nightline, Inside Edition*, and others) more and more people started hearing about what we were doing and many of them came to us for help. We met so many wonderful people with breathtaking stories.

Lights, Camera, Action

In the midst of all of this, we got an interesting offer. A TV production company contacted us, because they wanted to film a reality TV show that featured Tess, Savannah, and me. After talking it over, we agreed. I had always thought that filming would be fun and exciting. I didn't count on the hours of waiting around in the killer Arizona heat. I also didn't count on the difficulty of balancing friends, activities, two jobs, and school. Not only did the crews want to film the most important part of what we do, the exorcisms, but they also wanted to film us doing normal, everyday stuff. They shot us hanging out at the mall, doing karate, and horseback riding. We filmed for several weeks to create a pilot for the project, and I have never been so exhausted. Being on camera is grueling work. And then doing exorcisms on top of that was even more taxing physically, emotionally, and spiritually.

A typical day's schedule had me getting up early, putting on camera make-up and doing my hair (which I hate doing) and then running off to a filming location. Our cars were packed full of changes of clothing and enough beauty products to put Dolly Parton to shame. We would film for a couple of hours, and then I would run off to work a shift at my job or attend class, and then we would reconvene to shoot some more. We did have fun filming; we usually got rewarded with food and gelato which, of course, was consumed in front of the camera. We also had to do things over and over again in order to get different camera shots. One time the production company took us to our favorite mall to film us shopping, and they made us go up and down the escalator about fifteen times. Then, we had to do the same thing in the glass elevator. By the time we were done a small crowd had gathered to watch and we hurried off to the next location before we could catch a breath.

Another time we had to put on heels and walk back and forth on a dusty, unpaved road until they could get the shot in the right lighting. Then we would head over to a church to do exorcisms, working until the wee hours of the night, ministering to anyone who had demons and needed help. People flew in from all over the world to receive ministry, and we saw some spectacular things.

One of the most common questions that the girls and I ran into was: "You're so young, are you really mature enough psychologically and spiritually for this kind of work?" I think the people who ask these questions have these images in their heads of the three of us girls sitting in a room with a crazy person as we try to sort out mental issues. This is hardly the case. It's true, the girls and I are not health professionals with a Ph.D. in psychology. But since when do you need to have a doctorate to reach out to someone who is hurting and offer hope and comfort?

Tess, Savannah, and I are trained to deal with demons and inner healing, not mental health issues. And we don't attempt to do so. We never interfere with the treatment of a patient and we don't try to fix mental health problems. However, if there is a demon, the girls and I know what to do with that. Casting out demons is spiritual warfare. You don't have to be a psychologist to face down a demon and send it packing to hell. And the girls and I never cast out demons alone, we always have knowledgeable help nearby in the form of my dad and other experienced adults. It is also insulting to insinuate that someone who has demons automatically is mentally incompetent. We have worked with doctors, lawyers, psychologists, teachers and pastors. These are highly intelligent and educated people who are by no means crazy or mentally ill. Demons do not equal mental illness.

I believe that allowing an exorcism to be filmed accomplishes several things. First, it is a witness to those who don't know God, a testament to the power of God. Second, it is three young women being an example to others. Third, it lets people know that hope and help are available (while showing the dangers of messing around with the supernatural), and it reaches people who could never be reached otherwise.

By this time, my friends and I were getting to be pretty proficient at conducting exorcisms. We started doing more media appearances, both in the United States and overseas. Top international news stations picked up our story. We did stories with *National Geographic, Globo Brazil, 60 Minutes Australia, Good Morning America,* German and French television, and numerous print articles. We faced down the toughest, most cynical journalists. We had to have an answer ready for all challenges to our beliefs and actions. To be sure, it was not easy, but it proved to be very important to be forced to think through everything that we believed to make sure that it lined up with Scripture.

Through it all, I tried to keep my head. I had my Bible studies every day. I stayed in touch with friends and family, and I tried my hardest to lead a normal life. I would escape to ride my horse or head to a bookstore for a little bit, just to get some quiet time. While all of the exorcism training and media appearances were important, I also had to keep up with my schoolwork and activities. But it was worth it all.

I was becoming, whether I had planned it or not, a spiritual culture warrior. I realized I had been called by God to stand out from the crowd and openly battle the evil that was harming so many of my peers. I started to understand more deeply the serious spiritual problems that saturate the society I live in. Today's culture has been inundated with witchcraft and occult spirituality which has helped to open the door to exploring the supernatural.

The media and entertainment industry have been flooded with supernatural-themed books, TV shows, and movies. Witchcraft, occultism, vampirism, and Satanism are more popular than ever. People have always been curious about the supernatural realm, but now the door to the supernatural world has been thrown wide open. Too many people are walking through that door without a clue of what could be waiting on the other side.

People need to know and understand the truth about the unseen spiritual domain. They need to know that there are real consequences for messing around with the dark side of the supernatural. So, along with Tess and Savannah, I am spreading the word. This is why I take on the forces of darkness. I do it for God and for the thousands out there who are lost, who don't even know what they are doing is wrong. I want to stop the heartbreak and pain before it starts, before the enemy has a foothold in their lives.

CHAPTER 2

The Supernatural: A Powerful Magnet

The crowd of people, smashed together into some semblance of a line, had snaked its way around the amusement park. Young and old sweated under the summer's sun, eagerly awaiting their turn. The sun shone down with blinding intensity, and many held little portable fans in an effort to obtain relief from the blazing hot day. Hours passed, and still many waited patiently for a chance to experience a few brief minutes of excitement.

What could possibly be impressive and exciting enough to warrant hours standing outside under the hot sun? The highly acclaimed Harry Potter ride at Universal Studios. It follows young witches on broomsticks through a dark, twisting adventure as evil spirits (demons) torment Harry and his fellow occultists. Ghoulish-looking monsters are fended off with spells as the rider careens through dark rooms full of smog, video projections, and robotics. They almost feel as though they are flying alongside Harry and his wizard pals.

Known all over the world, the *Harry Potter* book series has become an international sensation, branching out from books to movies to theme parks. J.K. Rowling's brainchild has earned billions of dollars and people from every religion and country acclaim her work. The story chronicles the life of a young boy who possesses powers of wizardry and whose experiences are magical. While residing in a special place with other witches, he practices the art of sorcery and learns to hone his occult powers. The story depends on very dark supernatural dynamics and it is wildly popular, highly favored especially among teens and young adults.

Despite its blatant use of witchcraft and spell-casting (which is forbidden in the Bible), Harry-Potter-themed Bible studies and vacation Bible schools have popped up even among some Christian churches. Why do people have such a fascination with the supernatural and the occult? Why is there such intense curiosity about the unseen and unknown realm? Why would anyone want to stand in the hot sun for hours for a chance to ride a simulated broomstick like a witch? How is it, in fact, that one woman's imaginations could have translated into such a booming industry?

The answer is the inexorable pull of the supernatural. Children and adults will wait hours for only a few minutes' taste of a world beyond ours, of magic and mystical beings, and of epic battles between good and evil.

Is this attraction to the supernatural evil, or does it have a good underlying reason? The astounding answer, which almost takes your breath away, is because *we were created for such a world*. We are human beings who live in the natural, material world, but we all have a supernatural element to us. We were not created to live in this present world for eternity. When God made us, He created us as tripartite beings. We have a body, which is in the natural world, and we have a soul, which is the essence of each individual. We also have a spirit, which was made for greater things beyond this world.

When I say that we were made for a supernatural world, I don't mean a world of goblins and ghosts and wizards. I mean something much greater. We were made to live in the presence of God, as spiritual beings who delight in His holy presence. As Blaise Pascal said, "There is a God-shaped vacuum in the heart of every man which cannot be filled by any created thing, but only by God, the Creator, made known through Jesus." But when that hole is neglected, when God isn't fully there to fill it, we hunger to satiate it with something. And the Master Deceiver, Satan, knows this all too well and has provided tantalizing alternatives to God's presence in our lives. Sadly, the devil and the world he holds under his power have perverted that God-given spirituality.

Not only do people hurry all too often to fill that God-shaped hole with some other form of spirituality, but many people also suffer from generational curses that can create an added compulsion to experiment with things that are not of this world. When a young adult heads to the movie theater to see the latest installment in the *Harry Potter* or *Twilight* series, that curiosity and hunger for more than the natural world is temporarily satisfied, but it's a costly venture that only stimulates further explorations.

According to a Gallup poll, about three out of four Americans profess at least one paranormal belief. Throughout my time as a Teenage Exorcist, people have come to me with all kinds of questions about the supernatural and paranormal phenomena. In the following pages I will answer some of these questions to the best of my ability.

Exactly What Is "the Supernatural"?

The terms "supernatural" and "paranormal" are thrown around quite often as if everyone understands what they refer to. Merriam Webster defines *supernatural* as, "Of or relating to an order of existence beyond the visible observable universe; especially: of or relating to God or a god, demigod, spirit, or devil."

To an evolutionary psychologist, the belief in the supernatural is simply a cognitive tendency due to evolutionary processes. According to the American Psychological Association, psychologists recognize that children as young as three have a concept of a supernatural realm, but the only way they can explain this human notion about the existence of supernatural things is that it's been handed down within the human race; it's inborn.

Atheists' theories about supernatural things range from believing in absolutely no spiritual realm to believing in a supernatural world that has no deities.

Christians agree for the most part on the reality of a spiritual realm where God and His angels reside, along with some form of evil supernatural existence.

Virtually all religions believe in some form of the supernatural. From Islamic jinns (evil spirits) to Druidic witches conjuring spirits, the awareness of a realm outside of our natural world characterizes many different religions.

A general definition of the supernatural is that which is outside of the natural world. The prefix "super" refers to something "above and beyond." So the word supernatural literally means something that comes from beyond the natural world in which we live. The supernatural world is unseen by human eyes. God and His angels, along with Satan and his demons, all of whom are spirits, reside there. It is a spiritual realm. Practically speaking, "supernatural" and "paranormal" mean the same thing.

The Bible talks about the world that we cannot see, a place of angels, demons, heaven, hell, God, and Satan. However, the Bible makes it very clear that there is a veil between the natural and supernatural world. Not only can living people not cross that veil, neither can the dead. Once a person dies, his or her spirit cannot cross back to the earthly realm to haunt loved ones in the form of ghosts or apparitions. Rather, the spirits of those who die go to the Lord for judgment.

But some people will say, "I *saw* the ghost of my great-grandmother who died years ago!" How can that happen? It happens because, while God has forbidden necromancy and communicating with the dead, Satan has found a way to pervert this law. When ghosts make purported appearances, it is really demons masquerading as people who have died. By fooling someone into trying to communicate with a demon disguised as a loved one, Satan is able to open a doorway into the deceived person's life. Ruin and havoc follow.

So "the supernatural" refers to something that can't be explained by natural forces, something that is outside of the human perspective. We may not fully understand it because we may not be able to observe it with our five senses, but that does not disprove its reality.

What Is the Difference Between the Good and Bad Sides of the Supernatural?

What is the difference between a witch holding a séance and a pastor praying for angelic protection? Both are applying to supernatural forces for help, so what is the difference?

The distinction is that while the pastor is simply praying for what God has promised, the witch is doing what is clearly an abomination to the Lord. In two books of the Bible, Deuteronomy and Leviticus, God lays down clear, moral laws for His people. These are moral absolutes, absolute truths. God didn't arbitrarily lay down these laws because He felt like it; His intention is to protect His people from themselves. And part of the law that He laid down was a prohibition against supernatural, demonic entanglements. Because of the real and dangerous consequences of meddling in supernatural things, God sought to protect His people from allowing Satan to gain a foothold in their lives.

When God established His law, the Israelites had just come out of Egypt, which was a place rife with potent black magic. God knew that He had to provide His people with the dos and don'ts of involvement in the supernatural. Having created humans as spiritual beings, He understands better than anyone that our inborn fascination with the supernatural does not come with a natural ability to discriminate between the good side of the supernatural realm and the very dark side. God sought to protect the Israelites (and everyone, including us) from our own ignorance.

God made it very clear. He presented the two sides. On one side is God the Father, His Son Jesus, and the Holy Spirit, along with all the different Angels in Heaven—all goodness. On the other side is Satan and his demons, and hell, which is pure evil. God's mission is to redeem and love and liberate. Satan's mission is to kill and steal and destroy.

Therefore, very simply, if someone sins, which is to say someone transgresses God's divine law, that person opens the door to the dark side, to Satan. That is why God (speaking through Moses) said, "Give no regard to mediums and familiar spirits; do not seek after them, to be defiled by them: I am the Lord your God" (Leviticus 19:31). The devil's goal is to convince you to break God's commandments. Thankfully, you don't get a demon every time that you sin, but if he can get you involved in what God has expressly forbidden, you have consented to demonic oppression.

The problem is that so many people today are not aware that God has laid down His decrees and to violate them is to open oneself up to demonic attack. So often when I am working with those who have demons, they will look at me with tear-filled eyes and say, "I just didn't know what I was doing was wrong."

I wish for their sakes that ignorance could stand as a valid excuse for getting involved with the dark domain. However, as Paul tells us in his letter to the church at Rome:

> *For since the creation of the world His invisible attributes are clearly seen, being understood by the things that are made, even His eternal power and Godhead, so that they are without excuse, because, although they knew God, they did not glorify Him as God, nor were thankful, but became futile in their thoughts, and their foolish hearts were darkened.* (Romans 1:20–21)

To restate, the good side of the supernatural is within God's parameters. The bad side is anything that is outside of His commands. My rule of thumb is this: If in doubt, *don't.* It's not worth the risk.

Why Aren't People Repelled by the Evil Side of the Supernatural?

One would think that if the issue is as simple as good versus evil, it would seem pretty black and white. While we may understand that trying to communicate with the dead is evil and therefore shouldn't be attempted, we run into a multitude of seemingly gray areas, and that is where most people fall into trouble. It does not take long for people who are not turned off by supernatural evil to experience a deadening of their consciences.

One time I was talking with one of my best friends at college. We were discussing a popular TV show that we had watched. After a couple of episodes, I had stopped watching, disturbed by the graphic witchcraft and irreligious bent. I told her about my feelings, and she responded, "Sometimes I don't feel comfortable by what is being shown, but that doesn't stop me from watching it. I just don't feel *convicted* about watching it." I didn't know quite what to say. Why should she have to wait to feel convicted? She is a conservative Christian girl who understands that Satan is active and that evil is real, and yet she had no qualms about watching something that stood in blatant opposition to her beliefs.

This show was dark. Séances were held to summon evil spirits—authentic séances, complete with pentagrams, blood, and witchcraft. One of the main characters had sex with a demon that was animating a corpse, and angels were depicted as careless beings who gave no thought to wiping out entire cities and calling the human race parasites. These so-called angels even questioned the existence of God. Besides, even the demonology of the show was way off target. And this is just what you could see on the surface.

How could my friend watch this show season after season? It is because of a deadened conscience. She was relying only on the feeling of inner conviction to tell her if what she was doing was wrong. But feelings can lead one astray very easily. And it is never enough to expect guilty feelings to stop you from continuing to do something that you like. The Bible is very clear in its condemnation of the kinds of things portrayed on the show. I didn't need a feeling to tell me that it wasn't right. God's Word and His laws told me that it wasn't right.

It is possible to numb or "sear" your conscience as to what is right and wrong. The Bible mentions this: "Now the Spirit expressly says that in latter times some will depart from the faith, giving heed to deceiving spirits and doctrines of demons, speaking lies in hypocrisy, having their own conscience seared with a hot iron" (2 Timothy 4:2).

With only a little dabbling in the dark side of the supernatural, it is very easy to deaden one's conscience. It happens gradually, with a series of little transgressions, small pieces of ground conceded to the devil. These accumulate and hush that little voice in your head that whispers, "Don't go there." Easily enough, a young woman who is a strong Christian can deaden her conscience to the point of watching evil for the purpose of entertainment.

While a deadened conscience is one of the reasons why so many seem unaffected by the evil in the supernatural, there is another equally serious reason. We all live in a state of sin, fallen away from God and separated from Him. Humankind has been born into sin; we are fallen creatures. Our fundamental depravity compels us to seek out sin. No one is blameless; all have sinned. Romans 3:10 states, "As it is written: 'There is none righteous, no, not one.'" Our sinful natures keep pulling us toward the evil side of the supernatural. Just as the Israelites in days of old worshipped Baal and Ashtoreth and practiced all kinds of abominations, today humankind still sins right and left, thus opening the door to the dark side of the supernatural.

How Dangerous Can Involvement in the Supernatural Be?

Amanda was only fifteen when she was approached by a young man who claimed to be a Satanist. Despite having grown up in a Christian home with parents who loved her, Amanda was desperately unhappy. She wanted something more and had started searching for a cult to join. While she was in a local bookstore, a Satanist named James approached her and invited her to one of his meetings. She went with some trepidation, unsure of what was to come, unaware that years of hell on earth awaited her.

She was inducted into the group as a Satanist, and she even went so far as to be christened with a new satanic name, Lilith. After suffering through horrifying ceremonies full of unspeakable acts, she started working on her special skill set: Tarot card readings. Every member of the satanic cult was allowed to pick a talent to master, and Amanda chose Tarot cards. Tarot cards are a form of divination; they can supposedly tell the future, something that is forbidden by God. She went through spells and ceremonies to bind herself to the cards, even sleeping with them under her pillow.

Throughout her years as a Satanist, Amanda became proficient in her divination skills and she would even go into churches to stir up trouble. But she was miserable. One day, a miracle happened, and she found the Lord. After her conversion she ran, determined to leave her dark past behind her.

Fast forward twenty years later. Tess, Savannah, and I sat down with Amanda to help rid Amanda of her demons. She was a successful businesswoman who traveled all over the country representing a major corporation. But her life was falling apart. Already married and divorced, she fought a daily battle to keep going and she knew she had demons. She came to us desperate for help. I have never faced demons so vicious. It was one of the most harrowing exorcisms the girls and I have ever experienced.

Amanda is a tiny five-foot-one and she weighs almost nothing. She has a sweet disposition and looks like she would never hurt a fly. Yet it took five strong men to hold her back when the demons manifested. She had every demon you could imagine, and we fought for hours to win her freedom.

We had to go back through her life inch-by-inch, painstakingly, having her renounce any open door that she had given to Satan. And there were many doors. All along the way, the demons fought hard, and we had our hands full. They were extra-powerful because of the many legitimate holds they had on her life; she had essentially invited them to come in and stay.

She had demons from the Tarot card readings, she had demons from the satanic ceremonies that she had been subjected to, and she had demons from the witchcraft rites that she had performed. It was a hard spiritual battle, and we had a lot of ground to recover.

But God prevailed in the end. After we had canceled out every demonic stronghold in her life, we commanded the demons to leave her. They finally did so, with an ear-splitting scream. Then she slumped, exhausted after the ordeal. It was a very tough battle for all of us—tough because Amanda had given the evil spirits so much room to stand.

Apparently, Amanda's possession had all started when she played with an Ouija board when she was little. That opened the door to the demons and they only grew stronger as she grew older and gave them free reign in her life. Surely, those demons were what pulled her to Satanism and to the Tarot cards. That's how this works. Once the enemy gains a foothold in your life, all he has to do to strengthen his hold is to push you farther into sin.

With Amanda, regaining all that lost ground took a long, exhausting, sweaty battle. She is not the first person who has come to us after they have spent years messing around, expecting us to provide a quick fix. I usually have to tell them that there is no drive-thru deliverance. In fact, even after that initial session, which was ultimately successful, Amanda was far from free. We met with her again several more times and had to do several more deliverances to get rid of even more demons.

I tell Amanda's story because it is similar to countless others, and I want to warn everyone that I can about the dangers of getting involved with the dark side of the supernatural. After cleaning up so many broken lives that have been ruined when people unknowingly gave the devil a foothold in their lives, I want to shout: *It is not worth it!*

Beware, Satan Prowls About Like a Lion

No matter how cool or harmless it looks, playing around with the dark side of the supernatural is messy and dangerous. Having seen more than my fair share of hurt and pain, I know that Satan, the Master Deceiver, has learned how to make something look good that underneath is rotten. He will trap you. Satan was once a beautiful angel of light, glorious to behold, and look what he has become. You don't want to be near him, but don't let him deceive you into thinking that what he offers is still beautiful.

Don't succumb to his wiles because you are unaware; be sharp and on the lookout: "Be sober, be vigilant; because your adversary the devil walks about like a roaring lion, seeking whom he may devour" (1 Peter 5:8). Don't be a victim; be aware of the consequences of your actions. It is OK to be aware of the reality of the supernatural world, and it has a divine side of incredible beauty. But don't seek out the flip side, which is filled with great evil, a great evil that your sinful nature will gravitate to despite your better judgment. I don't want to meet with you someday because I have to clean up your life due to careless spiritual choices!

CHAPTER 3

The Media's Message

The media and the entertainment industry prove to be great barometers for revealing the interests of the public. When people are fascinated by supernatural things, the media quickly follows and feeds that fascination.

I'm sure that one of the reasons that reporters and representatives of the entertainment industry want to talk to Tess, Savannah, and me is because of that fascination; they want to hear our take on all things supernatural, because of our unique perspective. Not many teenagers can say they have stared into the face of evil and defeated it through God's power. And as all sorts of stories come to light about paranormal activities, fiction and nonfiction, we can act as stabilizers. We provide the other side of the stories that hold people enthralled—the truth side. In a world filled with evil and occult practices, we provide balance.

Even though my iPod is filled with all sorts of music from hip-hop to country, classical to pop, one of my favorite bands is Casting Crowns; I love all of their music. It is deep and it has meaning. I have several favorite songs, but one of my favorites is, "Slow Fade," which explains how the fall into sin is never a quick drop; it's a gradual and steady process. The descent into evil involves a series of incremental actions, which makes it harder to catch yourself when you start slipping. Many times people don't even realize how greatly they have erred or just how many concessions to sin they have made. The lyrics to "Slow Fade," based on the old gospel children's song, "Be Careful Little Eyes What You See," make an eloquent case for just how easy it is to fall into the devil's trap.

This is how the media and entertainment industry can affect us. I am not saying "the media" are inherently evil or have devious designs. Television, radio, the Internet, magazines, books, and movies merely provide a conduit for communicating information. It's the *message* in the media that can prove to be deadly for your soul. And while the entertainment industry certainly can be used for good, many times it serves as a hook to reel people into walking in step with Satan. The media can be a bit like a gateway drug. Once you let your eyes and ears take you through the door, you end up going deeper and farther than you expected, and soon you are hooked on something dangerous and deadly.

The fact is, once you get hooked on the supernatural, you want more. This is true for both the good and the bad. I am hooked on God's presence and the Holy Spirit. I hunger for more of God every day. I want to know all that I can about Him, and I want to experience Him. This is good; this is how God created us to be. But when people try to fill that God-hole in their lives with the bad kind of supernatural, it can be just as inviting; it invites evil in. Just as I invited good in when I asked Jesus to be my Savior, people can easily invite in evil.

Satan doesn't need much to start ruining your life. And he has found a great way to invade people's lives through the media.

It may start out with reading your favorite paranormal romance. Then before you know it, you are reading darker things than that first book. That may lead to playing around with automatic handwriting or spell-casting, and soon you start seeing dark shapes and begin having evil thoughts. Then you get visits by dark things that claim to be your friends, but they hurt you. Still you dig deeper, fascinated with this world of "make-believe romance." The more you give in, and the more concessions you make to evil, the more ammunition Satan has to attack you.

People who start out with innocent-seeming recreational reading may start pushing the boundaries. It's too easy to do, and I've seen it over and over again. This is why spiritual discernment is so important. The producers and publishers who aired your favorite TV show or published your favorite book series don't really care about your soul. They just want to push merchandise. If something makes money, they'll sell it. In the secular entertainment industry, anything goes. The people making the decisions represent a conglomeration of every belief out there, and many of them have bought into some pretty wacky ideas.

Is It Worth the Risk?

You have to be your own filter. Don't just take in whatever you see or read because it could lead you anywhere. Satan, who used to be an angel of light, knows how to make something look good. He knows that if evil doesn't look good or appealing on the outside no one will look at it. It is not paranoia to be careful. It's simply common sense.

The question to ask yourself when evaluating any form of media consumption or entertainment is: "Does this put me over the line that God has drawn between right and wrong?" A follow-up question is: "Is it worth it?" No book or movie, no matter how inviting it looks, is worth the risk of demonic oppression. Why would you want to open the door to the dark side of the supernatural?

As I have learned more and more about spiritual warfare, my thinking has evolved. I started out trying to figure out how much I could get away with, trying to calculate just how close I could get to the bad side without crossing the line that God has drawn. Now, after doing countless exorcisms and seeing the consequences of spiritually rebellious actions, I have changed. Now I think like a spiritual warrior. I have looked into the face of true evil. I have seen families torn apart and destroyed by the devil and his demons, and I want no part of it in my own life. I don't want to give the devil any foothold.

I think like a spiritual warrior because I am in a battle. All of us are. We are embroiled in a spiritual war whether we know it or not. Just because we can't see it doesn't mean this supernatural war isn't going on. We choose sides by our decisions and actions.

Any military general will tell you that it's easier to hold ground than to try to recover it after it has been taken. That's why God warns us not to let Satan get his foot through the door. Remember what 1 Peter 5:8 says: "Be sober, be vigilant; because your adversary the devil walks about like a roaring lion, seeking whom he may devour."

Have you given Satan room to operate in your life? Have you made concessions to the Evil One? Have you ventured further than you should have into the dark side of the supernatural world? Have you allowed the media's messages to seduce you?

What Is True?

So many people take as truth whatever they see or hear through the media. "Well, it's on the news, so it must be true," is their mindset. But of course "truth" is not really the goal of secular broadcasters, producers, or publishers—money is.

The list of the two hundred all-time top-grossing movies in the world includes *The Exorcist, Harry Potter,* and *Twilight. The Exorcist* grossed over two hundred million dollars. The Harry Potter franchise is worth fifteen billion dollars and still counting. Even extremely low-budget films such as *Paranormal Activity,* which cost only fifteen thousand dollars to make but yielded over a hundred and eight million, show the market allure of supernatural-themed movies. The facts are in the figures. It's financially advantageous for media companies to exploit this fascination with the paranormal. None of them is concerned about the eternal value or the truth of what is being shown. The bottom line is in the cash, and if something will sell, it will be produced and sold.

Besides money, another motivation for Hollywood is plain old curiosity. Behind the cameras are producers and directors, writers and network CEOs who are ordinary people, created by God the same way as you and I. Like everyone else, they long to fill the spiritual part of their souls and spirits. Most of them do not know how to do that; all they know is that they are curious about anything supernatural. Their ranks are filled with people who profess every kind of belief and religion out there, and very few are atheists. Many believe in some form of the supernatural, which is why the New Age is so popular. Many of them are very creative, and more curious than the average person, eager to inquire into new things. This aids their work. And it gets them in trouble. Even when they understand that something supernatural is evil, they don't shy away from it.

One day, my father was in a meeting with some of the top Hollywood screenwriters and producers. As he was leaving the meeting, he was approached by a man in attendance. Dad was late for his flight and couldn't stay to talk, but the man begged for a couple of minutes. He said, "Hey, I know you don't know me, but I'm one of the biggest writers in Hollywood. I sit in my office all day, and I write horror scripts. Listen, I know there's something really evil behind all this; I just don't know what it is. Can you tell me what it is?" He was a successful horror script writer who was an expert at portraying evil in supernatural flicks. But he did not know that Satan was serving as his muse.

Don't be fooled into complacency even if you are a Christian. Never underestimate your enemy. Satan is clever and crafty. He will use whatever he can to ensnare you. While the media can be used for good, great evil prevails. Don't use the cheap excuse that you only watch or read something questionable because of its entertainment value. Don't believe the lie that as long as you don't believe it or support it, you'll be fine. That's just what the enemy wants you to think.

If you think that you can watch or read whatever you want just because you have some special sort of impunity, then go ahead. Go ahead and watch porn, read the *Satanic Bible*, indulge in whatever you want. Because, hey, you don't believe it anyway; it's just for entertainment. But let me caution you—your intent doesn't matter, because it's your actions that count.

Satan doesn't care if you believe in demons and hell or not. He doesn't care what you believe. He only cares about hooking you into the dark side of the supernatural. As you are exposed to many messages from the media every day, you can decide which ones you will listen to. You can decide which ones you will let into your life and thoughts.

The media is very powerful. Be aware and beware.

CHAPTER 4

Never a Dull Moment!

As one of the Teenage Exorcists, I have met with and interviewed with some of the top names in the media world. As I explained in the previous chapter, today's entertainment industry provides a gateway into the supernatural world, and they provide a glimpse into its mysteries, whether accurate or not. Because of media fascination with the paranormal, our story intrigues them. I love the fact that it's atheists and non-believers who are helping us spread the gospel because they are so curious about three teenage girls taking on the forces of darkness. Besides stirring interest because of what we do, Tess, Savannah, and I break every stereotype: We are young, we are girls, and we are passionate about the Lord and helping people. And largely because of the media interest, we are able to continue to do what we do.

Of course it has proven to be a mixed blessing. Because of media attention, we have been able to minister to and reach larger numbers of people that we could have reached otherwise. But at the same time, the same media have spread nasty rumors far and wide. Every aspect of who we are has been attacked and ridiculed. We have worked with print and film crews who were courteous and easy to work with, while others have been surly and cynical. I feel privileged to have been allowed to see "behind the scenes," and I know how members of the media construct a story. If nothing else, one thing has become abundantly clear—the media wield enormous power in today's world.

I have seen firsthand how a story can be twisted and prodded to fit the show's angle and how easy it is to take anything out of context. I have had some outrageous claims made about me. People have made many errors, from spelling my name wrong to claiming that I never watch movies or that my dad is a southern Texas preacher. However, we know that when we agree to film with a crew we are taking a chance. We know that there is always a real possibility that we could be ridiculed or mocked. But we usually go ahead and agree to work with both print and film producers because of the results. Who knows who is viewing our media appearances or reading the articles about us? Who knows how many viewers and readers have been touched?

After our names appear someplace, we get emails from all over the world, from all sorts of people, asking questions, asking for help, and asking for prayer. People have flown in from all over the world to get help, simply because they saw us on TV or in a magazine. By working with secular shows we are able to quite effectively witness to people who have never heard the gospel message before. We film with the crews and let them watch us work, and then we leave the results up to God.

Changed Lives

Sometimes it's the crew members themselves that we reach. One time we were filming with the Travel Channel in an office building. The girls and I were simply telling our story, when the main cameraman suddenly put down his camera and said, "Guys, I'm feeling something." We stopped everything and went over to him as he knelt on the ground. He was inexplicably shaking and sick to his stomach and he struggled to curb his groundless anger. He looked up at us, and when I got a good look in his eyes I knew that whatever was in him was reacting to us as we talked about our ministry.

I asked some questions to find out more, and as we talked, several important details came up. He was, in his own words, "a raging alcoholic," and he talked about having had a very rough start growing up. His current job was investigating and filming supernatural and paranormal sightings all over the country. This had led him to some very dark locations, and he had witnessed many demonic ceremonies. Even though he was only there because it was an assignment and he was supposed to maintain an investigative perspective, he had been deeply affected by what he had seen and experienced.

One day, as he was driving away from filming he had caught a glimpse of something dark and evil in his rearview mirror, following him home. Somehow he knew that he had picked up some demons. His struggles with rage and alcoholism grew worse, and he felt that there was a malignant presence in his life.

Now, as we worked with him, it all came bubbling to the surface. I anointed him with oil, and we confronted the demons in him that we knew were there. With a growl and hate-filled glare, they manifested. The chief demon was vicious and was firmly entrenched in this man's life.

We discovered that by being a part of occult ceremonies and going to haunted locations where paranormal signs had occurred, this man had unknowingly opened himself up to demons. They had taken full advantage of his lapses with alcohol, and he was suffering a miserable life.

Thankfully, somehow, he had been chosen to film our story. He knelt down as we worked to cast the demons out of his life for good. After we broke off all demonic strongholds in his life and had the demons renounce their right to this man, we commanded the demons to come out of him and return to the pit of Hell. With a yell that we hoped wouldn't bring cops running to our door, the demons left. And then we ran for a bucket as he started throwing up, physically expelling the evil that had been tormenting him. As he recovered, absolute joy took over. He seemed as if a huge weight had just been lifted off his life. Whereas he had walked into the office building a defeated man, he left joyous in his newfound freedom.

A year or so later, we got a call from this same crew-member. He was a changed man. He shared that after he received ministry his life had taken a miraculous turn for the better. He was happy and had quit his addiction to alcohol as well. No longer tormented, he had found peace. He found it in an unlikely place! God loved him and made sure that he crossed paths with us, because we would be able to help him in a way that no one else could.

Dan from the BBC

The third year of our ministry found Tess, Savannah and I traveling almost everywhere. It was our last summer before college together and we wanted to savor every moment. We were approached by someone from BBC-TV, the largest news organization in the world, headquartered in London, England. They wanted to film a documentary on the Teenage Exorcists. Dan was the man in charge of the production and he would be following us, documentary-style, to capture on camera what we do. The contract called for six months of shooting, and there was the possibility of going to London to wrap up the documentary. We were ecstatic, with our love of all things British (and I am a huge Doctor Who fan).

Filming started January of that year, with Dan coming to visit the girls and me in Arizona, where we live. His goal was to film us doing everyday, "normal" stuff. (This seems to happen with every crew; they always want to be sure to show our conventional side to the world.) So we ride our horses and go shopping and do karate for the camera. The fun shots are important in that they add human interest, but that's not why we allow them to film us doing these things. Our real passion is reaching out to the lost and brokenhearted.

So we rode horses in the sweltering Arizona heat, we practiced karate in the middle of the day in my backyard, and Tess played the piano with great aplomb. "Normalcy" established, we headed to Pasadena, California, where Dan could watch us in action at a seminar. That same day Tess and I had been competing at a high school debate tournament in the same city, so we arrived at the seminar location having already clocked a fourteen-hour day.

When we arrived, Dan was there, ready to interview us before the seminar, and he had some very interesting questions. "What exactly is Satan and what are his demons?" He asked as we scurried around trying to get ready. This is a question that we get asked a lot, and it's an important one.

We gave him our summary-style answer: "When God created the world, it was beautiful and perfect, there was no Satan or hell, no pain, and no evil. One of God's mightiest angels was named Lucifer; he was glorious to behold and extremely powerful. But pride had gotten the best of Lucifer, and he thought he could exalt himself higher than the Lord. So he rebelled against God, trying to usurp Him, and God threw him out of heaven.

"Jesus mentioned this when His disciples came to him. They were astonished that they could cast out demons in His name and asked Him about it. 'He replied, "I saw Satan fall like lightning from heaven."' When Satan (who is the same as Lucifer) rebelled, one third of all of the angels in heaven followed him and were cast out of Heaven with him. These fallen angels became demons.

"Then when Jesus died on the cross, in one stroke He defeated Satan and death. That is how we can cast out demons, Christ has given us the authority to do so, and Satan has already been defeated. We just have to enforce our victory over him."

While all of this might be common knowledge to a Christian, it was brand-new information to Dan, as it usually is to the people in our audiences.

Dan asked us if we should try to "save" the demons we come across in deliverance. "Absolutely not!" we replied. "Demons have no redeeming qualities, for they are pure evil and cannot be saved. They threw in their lot with Satan a long time ago, and nothing can change them. Demons are evil spirits, which means they are incorporeal and are supernatural beings. We need to beware of them because, like Satan, demons know how to make evil look good. So when someone thinks he can talk to Grandma who is in her grave, he is really communicating with a heinous evil spirit disguised as a loved one. In fact, in almost every deliverance that we do, the demons laugh outright in glee at the suffering and pain they have inflicted on their victim. They deserve the torment of God for their perfidy, not a second chance."

With this explanation in hand, Dan filmed us that evening as we ministered to many people. We worked late into the night, dealing with demons of hate and abuse along with a couple of Jezebel and witchcraft spirits. At midnight, we called it a night and packed up to head back to the hotel, for Tess and I had a full day of competing at the debate tournament the next day. We got back to the hotel by two in the morning and slept for a few hours before it was time to get up to compete again.

We were glad to know that Dan's perspective on good and evil had been changed permanently in the right direction.

The Makeup Artist

In the midst of this shoot, Tess, Savannah, and I made friends with a wonderful makeup artist who did our makeup for shoots. She was a sweetheart, and we had gotten to talk and hang out in the hours between filming. At her first shoot with us, after hearing that we cast out demons, she asked to stay and watch. It was a very dramatic exorcism, and she was shaken. Although this young woman didn't believe in God, she had just seen a demon manifest and get cast out by the power of God.

The next time we saw her, she was different. She glowed and was happier than she had been in a long time. When we talked, she admitted that seeing the exorcism that night had really made her think about her life and relationship with God. She had some very deep conversations with her family, and they made some changes in their lives. She had been changed by what she saw, for she had been forced to face the truth of there being a real and evil presence in the world.

Then, months later, we got an emergency call from her. Things had gone south fast, and she was calling from a hospital, having just tried to kill herself. We were shocked. This was so out of character for the precious lady that we knew, and as she told us everything that had recently happened in her life, we knew that something supernatural—something dark—was going on.

We met with her the next day. Dad was out of town on a trip, so it was up to us three girls to get to the bottom of what had happened. We talked and prayed and eventually that night we cast out a vicious demon of Death. This demon had been working her whole life to kill her and had almost succeeded. If she hadn't come to us to get rid of that demon, she would have died one day. She didn't even know that she had a demon. That's why we have a saying in our ministry: "Get your stuff, before your stuff gets you."

Her story is a great example of how God uses the most unlikely means to accomplish His purposes. A non-Christian makeup artist was on our shoot, met us, saw an exorcism, and then knew where to go to get help when she needed it. I am so thankful that this young woman knew she could come to us. God cared about her enough to put us into her life months before she would recognize that she needed it.

CHAPTER 5

Out of My Comfort Zone

Throughout the months of the BBC documentary filming, I had an idea percolating in the back of my head. Although I have traveled extensively with my dad, Tess and Savannah had never been with me on a mission trip. I love to travel. I knew that if I could talk everyone into going and get a trip together, it would take our ministry experience to the next level. I had toured Eastern Europe with my family a few years before. Ukraine and Russia were two of the places we visited, and I never forgot that trip and the miracles I had seen as Dad did exorcisms all over the country. I wanted to go back and bring my best friends with me so that we could reach the youth of Ukraine, Russia, and beyond with a message of freedom and deliverance. The people in the region are hungry for God, and many are in deep demonic oppression. I wondered if I could pull together a trip.

After many phone calls and emails, we did it! We were able to coordinate a trip to Eastern Europe! We soon found ourselves headed to Ukraine and Russia. Dan was still filming with us for the BBC, and he decided to come along for part of the trip to capture what an overseas mission is like. We also agreed to let a media crew from an entertainment company called VICE follow us to do a story. We knew that VICE was an internet sensation, but we were unaware at the time of how cynical this entertainment company really is.

This trip had two important goals: this was our first international trip together and we were going to be followed by these big media companies. We were excited to be able share our testimony so widely, and we knew it would prove to be exhausting.

Pressing Needs

In other parts of the world, places where American Christian legalism has failed to put a damper on the casting out of demons, exorcists receive an eager reception. Our itinerary in Eastern Europe was jam-packed. We were going to be touring and ministering in Ukraine and Russia and ministering in one of Europe's largest Bible colleges. In partnership with a European church, we set our sights on reaching as many people in Ukraine and Russia as we could. Dad was going with us to help us minister.

We traveled to Ukraine first, arriving in Kiev after almost two days of flights. We met our Ukrainian friends there, then piled into a car for a four-hour drive to Kharkov. Upon arriving, we went out to eat (they loved feeding us there, and we didn't complain) and then crashed in a small apartment that was loaned to us for the night.

We had a day or so before the film crews would be arriving and things would get really crazy, so we were able to tour the city a bit before our first conference session that evening. We encountered delectable sushi, questionable subway rides, and pigeons that had been dyed pink and green for photo ops. Then before we knew it, it was time for our first seminar.

Thousands of people were crammed into an old Soviet-era theater. The place was packed, and I was really nervous. I had never spoken before such a large crowd before, and I had never worked with an interpreter either. Thankfully I had Tess and Savannah by my side.

I will never forget that first heart-wrenching night of ministry, and I will never forget the faces in the crowd. We walked onto the stage into blinding lights, and it took a moment for my eyes to adjust. When they did, I saw that the room was overflowing. People were everywhere, some even sitting in the aisles, many of them about my age. Miraculously, I wasn't nervous anymore, only eager to share my story. The three of us talked for a bit, exhorting the Ukrainian youth to learn how to fight spiritual warfare and to understand how the supernatural world works. Ukraine is a place rife with witchcraft and oppression, and our message was clearly grasped by the people because of their personal exposure to the dark side of the supernatural. Nobody in the room had ever tasted the candy-coated version of spiritual freedom that many American Christians are fed.

When we started the time of ministry, Savannah led out with a call for those in the audience who wanted to learn more about spiritual warfare and the supernatural. We weren't prepared for half of the audience to get up and rush the stage! This was a raw hunger, and we could see how much they wanted what we had. They had no trouble recognizing the evil in the world and they had no difficulty believing that the evil comes from a very real enemy to humanity: Satan. They wanted to learn how to fight against this enemy of God. They also wanted personal freedom from the bondage of the dark side of the supernatural.

In order to minister to as many people as we could, we spread out, sharing only one interpreter among the three of us. We were casting out demons, and we were also there to minister in any way we could. We were pulled this way and that. People wanted prayer and they wanted us to anoint them. I prayed, hugged, and cried with the brokenhearted as I struggled to make sense of what was going on.

People shoved pictures of loved ones in my face, begging me to pray over the photo, while others cried from the torment of old soul wounds that had surfaced.

I always carry my Bible, special cross and anointing oil with me and I had to watch out for people who wanted to take them and use them on people. As soon as we started confronting demons, the demons manifested and people commenced howling all over the audience. The theater was a scene of utter chaos. The stage was so filled with people that we could barely walk through the press of bodies. With the significant language barrier, we tried to find anyone who could even speak a few words of English to help interpret what was going on. People would grab me and place my hands on them for help. I was crying as I prayed with people, I was so touched and humbled by both their pain and their desperate hope. I was even able to cast out a few demons too.

All too soon it was time to go. We had rented out the theater for a certain amount of time and when that time was up, everything would be shut off. We had to leave, and it was terrible. The people begged us to stay. We three girls couldn't extricate ourselves, so we had bodyguards make a wall around us as we walked, pushing us out the door. As I walked out, people were still grabbing onto me, pleading for prayer. It was the hardest thing to walk away, with my heart bleeding for all of those frantic people. Their need was so great.

There was something in that room that is scarce in America—a sharp awareness of the spiritual battle being fought. The people knew they were under spiritual attack, and they wanted to do something about it. I wish more people had that point of view in America. I can too easily forget that most Christians aren't like me, because almost every week I come face to face with evil, and there's no escaping the reality of Satan and his demons. But for many American Christians, spiritual warfare has become an antiseptic thing. Say a prayer and then go on about your day.

Spiritual warfare needs to be so much more than that because the devil's evil is so sinister. You know you are facing unadulterated malice when you stare into the eyes of evil and listen as demons explain their bone-chilling plans for the Christians you are ministering to. Spiritual warfare takes on a whole new dimension when you face down demons who are giggling in glee at the pain they have inflicted. American Christians need to wake up, seriously. Ukraine and Russia have been waking up, and that's why their dearly-fought victories over the devil that night were so sweet.

After that night, my resolve was fired. Throughout the rest of our Ukrainian/Russian trip, we doubled our efforts to equip and educate people on the nature of supernatural evil. We wanted to stop them before they made mistakes. We wanted to stop their heartbreak and pain before it carried them deeper into the darkness. I hope that we were able to accomplish that, we certainly tried our best. I was doubly thankful that the members of the media were there, because they got to witness our efforts too, and they carried the story of our trip to millions of viewers.

Bible College Diary

There were times when, after a full day of travel and ministry, we would get called out of our beds to go meet someone at the church who needed help. Then there were times when I would try to catch a few minutes of sleep on a bumpy Ukrainian country road as we were ferried from place to place. (In all my travels, I have picked up the talent of falling asleep anytime and anywhere, which can be a help or a hindrance, depending on the situation.)

My favorite part of the trip was the Bible college that we stopped at for a few days. It was a home to hundreds of students, and the people at the college worked with a substance abuse rehabilitation center. This particular branch of the church was doing wonderful things in the community. We had the opportunity to speak to hundreds of seminary and college students about supernatural things. We warned them about knowing the difference between the good and bad sides of the supernatural realm and we showed them God's power through exorcisms. It was at this point in our trip that the two media companies, VICE and the BBC, caught up with us to see us in action.

Our days at the Bible college were hectic. We would get up early and head right to the church, staying there until well into the night. Ukrainian people are the most hospitable hosts, and the food was unbelievably good. Every time we would get back from a speaking session, a full three-course meal was laid out for us. We sometimes had up to five meals a day, not to mention the chocolates and desserts that came at us from every direction.

We would pull into the church in the early morning and head upstairs for first breakfast. Already we could hear the worship music pumping. Then we would go out and teach a session, arriving back in the green room afterward, all pumped up, to find second breakfast laid out. The film crews would try to work in interviews throughout the day, especially at mealtimes, so we didn't have a second off. Then we would head back out onto the stage where Tess, Savannah, and I would teach the youth about our paranormal and supernatural experiences.

When we got back to the green room again, we would have lunch and chocolates in between interviews and meeting with people who had demons. Then it was back to the stage again for our last teaching session of the day. At the end, we would sign books for people, pray with them and get them ready for the exorcism rally that night.

Back in the green room, we would have first dinner and spend some time preparing for the night rally. I often did some research on the region and the kinds of demons that I had faced earlier, so that I would be ready for the night.

The last night, as we prepared to go onstage for the final seminar night, the three of us had to stop and regroup. It had been a harrowing day, tiring emotionally, spiritually, physically, and intellectually. Our eyes were beginning to droop, and I had already fallen half-asleep during first dinner. As we looked at each other, worn out by the hectic days, we could see firm determination in each other's eyes, behind the jet-lag-induced haze. We had all been mightily impacted by what we had experienced during the past few days. Amidst the craziness of all the action and excitement, we had been able to connect with some amazing people. The youth were especially taken with the idea that they too could learn about spiritual warfare and how to distinguish between the good and bad of the supernatural.

What struck me the most was that almost everyone wants to do the right thing, but when it comes to the supernatural, many just don't know what the right thing is. And that is where my friends and I came in. In our work, we are showing people how to tell the difference between the good and bad of the supernatural. We are showing first-hand what can happen if one ignores God's warning about the dark side of the supernatural. Seeing people screaming and writhing in demonic torment is a very convincing deterrent to sin!

Charlot

Then there was Charlot. She was the host for the VICE camera crew, and she was a hurting woman. We know she was touched by what she saw in Ukraine; I could see it clear as day. But she turned her back on it all. I liked her, stoic Brit that she was, and in our brief time together I enjoyed getting to know her. She had a fascinating story and had traveled all over the world. But there was thinly concealed pain in her past, and I could tell she hadn't had a very pleasant life.

In our interviews with her, she could not seem to believe our sincerity in what we do. She thought there must be a hidden angle, some ulterior motive. She was especially nonplussed by how we lived our personal lives. She couldn't believe that we were rebellion-free teenagers who sincerely didn't want to get mixed up with the wrong crowd. We lived by what we preached, and she didn't know quite what to make of it. Since she could not believe what she was seeing with her own eyes, she simply dismissed our sincerity as empty-headed vapidness. When the documentary came out, she dismissed us as attention-seeking virgins who didn't know any better. She made it seem as if we lived in this bizarre bubble, cut off from the outside world. She knew better. She had seen the truth and God's power, but instead of embracing it, she ran back to a place of safety where she wouldn't have to face the implications of what she had experienced in Ukraine.

I'm sad about Charlot, for from what I could tell, she was affected by being around us. When my father prayed for her at one point, she started shaking and seemed almost paralyzed. And her eyes. When dad prayed over her and confronted her demons, I could see the evil in her eyes. There is a very strong chance that she has demons. The tragedy is that instead of getting help and opening herself up to the truth, Charlot stayed behind her safe walls of disbelief and darkness.

Sad to say, that is exactly what so many people do when faced with an uncomfortable truth. They run away. To face the consequences of their wrong actions and beliefs is just too much for some to handle. They are like Charlot, who was shaken from her sarcastic, disparaging position, yet instead of embracing what was right before her eyes, retreated behind her safe walls of cynicism and atheism. There is safety in the familiar, in things that don't challenge you. Some people have trouble accepting the bold reality of exorcism because it is uncomfortable for them, probably because they have a few skeletons hiding in their own closets.

Exorcism cuts to the root of problems and forces people to face some unpleasant truths. That's why they think it's a bad thing. But that's good! Who wants junk and demons if it is not that difficult to get rid of them? It may take some courage to face your demons, but it's true that freedom is right around the corner.

People who don't believe in God and who disparage exorcism have put themselves into a different kind of difficulty. When atheists and agnostics come and watch what we do, it puts them into a bit of a quandary. They may have witnessed an actual demon manifesting in a person, a demon who knows things nobody in the room knows, who has supernatural strength, and who sometimes even speaks in foreign languages! That kind of thing is pretty hard to dismiss as anything but a supernatural occurrence. Not only that, but they watched that same evil, snarling demon get cast out by God through a teenage girl.

That's a lot to wrap your head around if you happen to think this God stuff is a bunch of baloney. So the knee-jerk response I most often see is the person's complete denial of everything he or she has just witnessed. It is a panicked reaction of a person who refuses to accept what his or her own eyes have seen. If unbelievers should accept as fact what they have witnessed personally—real demons being cast out by the power of a real God—then they must face the realization that there is in fact a God. For many, that represents too great a leap outside their faith-repudiating comfort zone.

So all we can do is to present the truth and demonstrate the reality of the Kingdom of God pushing out the kingdom of darkness. Although I have been trained as a debater and so has Tess, and we would love nothing more than to state our convincing arguments about the reality of Satan and his demons, as well as God, we can't do that (and it doesn't work if we try). We have had to make our peace with doing our best in ministry and leaving the rest up to God. At least we know that we are leaving it in capable hands!

Aspiring Exorcists

That last day in Ukraine, after gulping down a couple of Ukrainian energy drinks, we hit the stage with renewed urgency. The night went well. People really listened to what we had to say. We were not exhausted anymore, possibly from the power of the message—or maybe only from the energy drinks.

When it came time to confront the demons in the audience, the room erupted in pandemonium. People who were manifesting demons were brought to the stage as quickly as possible and we tried to get to them all.

Then we did something that we don't do very often.

Dad invited the young people in the room to come up and help us cast the demons. A huge group rushed the stage, and we began to teach them how to confront the devil. It was eye-opening and liberating for many. For perhaps the first time, they were looking into someone's eyes and not seeing the person, but the demon lurking behind. And they got the chance to confront that evil, to make it leave and to stand up to Satan. This was a powerful experience. So many students were given the chance to go directly into battle for God! The excitement in the air was palpable as Ukrainian teenagers fearlessly confronted snarling demons.

As I rushed about helping aspiring exorcists, Savannah encountered someone whose life had been held in bondage because of psychics. She had been praying with someone when she was called to the side of a young girl for help. This girl had been brought up onstage because she was crying and had felt something stir when Dad had confronted the crowd's demons. But despite everyone's best efforts, there was no further manifestation of a demon. Savannah calmed the girl down and started talking with her, trying to find out more.

To Savannah's astonishment, this young woman revealed that her own mother had tried to kill her multiple times when she was growing up! Her tale of woe didn't end there, for she had also suffered other kinds of abuse throughout her life. In desperation, she had sought out psychics, but to no avail. When Savannah heard about the psychics, she got a hunch. Whipping out her anointing oil, Savannah anointed the middle of the girl's forehead, which to psychics and New Age mediums is known as the psychic third eye. In witchcraft and Eastern religions, it's the focal point of spiritual energy and all knowledge and enlightenment. It's an evil substitute for the presence of the Holy Spirit guiding us. When this young girl had gone to the psychic, this third eye had been "opened," which had allowed more demons into her life.

The minute Savannah's oil touched her forehead, the girl let out a shriek that shook the whole building. I remember being across the room and whipping my head around at the nerve-shredding sound. She started fighting and screaming as the demons finally manifested. It took four men to hold her. Her demons were very strong and powerful because of the abuse and witchcraft. But Savannah didn't give up and after an hour-long battle, the demons were cast out of her. This poor young girl had never had a chance against these demons. She did not know that she wasn't supposed to go to a psychic. All she knew was that she needed help. We did our best to give her the real help she needed so badly.

This girl helped show why what Tess, Savannah, and I do is so important. We are offering real solutions to pain and torment. We can explain why you don't have to go to a witch or psychic for relief and how to come to the God who created you and who can save you. It's ironic (and sad) to see that when people seek out the dark side of the supernatural for help they end up getting pushed even further away from getting set free. Instead of fixing their problem, their efforts merely compound it and create a bigger mess.

We must keep spreading the good news!

CHAPTER 6

Hear No Evil, See No Evil

Anna Marie had been raised in the church. She grew up loving Jesus and was a perfect angel for her parents. One day, while on a college getaway, she and her friends decided to play some old-fashioned paranormal games in the living room. They played Light as a Feather and Bloody Mary and a few other seemingly innocuous games. Then as a joke, they held a fake séance with each girl taking turns pretending to be the medium and communicating with "spirits" to find out who would marry whom and what type of car they would be driving when they were fifty. Despite a few niggling doubts, Anna Marie threw herself into the games, not wanting to be the church prude of the group who ruined the fun. They went home the next day and things were normal, for a while.

But one day as Anna Marie was sitting on her bed in her dorm, studying with her roommates, her world was rocked.

She was engrossed in one of her books when suddenly the mattress she was sitting on got ripped out from underneath her, and she was flung against the wall. She sat up, dazed, her roommates mirroring her expression of shock. No one had been near enough to Anna Marie to even touch the mattress, but somehow she had been flipped off her bed, and her mattress lay crumpled off to the side. It was as if a strong, unseen force had flipped her, trying to injure her. Shaken, Anna Marie did the only thing she knew to do—she prayed—gradually calming down and eventually dismissing the inexplicable event.

But that wasn't the end. A couple of months later, she was at her parent's house and she went into the bathroom to freshen up for dinner. She walked in the door, flipped on the lights and froze in terror. In the shower lay the crumpled shower curtains. A dark shape, almost like a black cloud, larger than a man, loomed over her. Paralyzed with fear, she watched as it reached out to touch her. A dark, evil laugh filled the room. Flinging herself out of the bathroom, she screamed "Jesus!"

Something was really wrong. She was scared and she knew that something evil was after her. She went to her childhood pastor, but after listening to her with a kind smile on his face, he rebuffed her concerns and her bizarre-seeming tale. He told her that she simply needed to pray the darkness away and it would leave. She tried that, and she started going to church weekly. The demonic activity continued and seemed to be stepping up. Frantic, she went to other pastors, trying to get help, but everyone thought she was crazy or that she was imagining things. When she asked if demons could be the cause, she received patronizing smiles and platitudes.

Desperate, she finally went to go see a healer who claimed he could help. The healer was a very nice older man who was pleasant and genuinely concerned for her. He agreed that something was going on, and he came to her house to pray over it and perform some incantations and rituals to drive the "evil forces" away. Anna Marie allowed it. She was desperate enough to try anything. For a while after the healer came, things quieted down. But as soon as she turned back in the direction of the church, the strange experiences started up again.

Tormented and at the end of her rope, she finally came to us. We were not surprised that she had not received much help from the church or the pastors. Instead of providing a safety line for people floundering in the misery of spiritual torment, the church will all too often give you the phone number of the nearest psychiatrist. Now this is not always true. There are pastors who will courageously try to help the people who come to them, but many are unequipped for the task. A large number of pastors and church leaders have been taught that once you're saved, the spiritual battle is over; Satan can never touch you again, and if you are struggling spiritually, you are just fighting against "the flesh," which often gets blamed for everything from sin to demonic activity. Many of the people I have worked with feel that the church treats them as if they are crazy for thinking that demons are bothering them.

Never mind that exorcisms are found throughout the New Testament, performed by Jesus and His disciples. It was integral to the life of the early church. Jesus and the early Christians did not intone placating prayers, but rather effected outright deliverance from demonic possession. Exorcism has biblical precedent. Nowadays, at least in most of the Western church, many pastors see no need for deliverance. Sometimes they denigrate it as primitive and crude. Other times, it is just too messy and inconvenient and hard to undertake. For many people, confronting the evil forces directly demands (and often reveals) too much.

Becoming a Christian does not automatically fix all of your problems. I wish it did, but people's problems do not just go away when they confess Christ as Lord and Savior. Of course, Satan wants Christians to be lured into a false sense of security, so that he can wreak havoc in their lives, unimpeded. How can you successfully stand against an enemy that you don't think exists? How can you fight spiritual warfare if you believe that you are immune to evil because of a simple salvation prayer?

The results are in: Christians don't have it any easier than the rest of the world. In fact, we have it rougher because we have declared ourselves enemies of Satan by believing in God. Christians have a target on their backs; Satan wants to bring us down. For while he cannot steal our salvation, he can try to turn earth into a living hell for us. All too often, we blindly cooperate with him.

God warns us that we will be persecuted: "All who desire to live godly in Christ Jesus will suffer persecution" (2 Timothy 3:12). Therefore, we need to know our enemy and be prepared for attacks. And yet for the most part, Christians are remiss in learning spiritual warfare. I have seen good, godly Christians living hellish lives for seemingly no reason. Satan can attack finances, relationships, health, and emotions if someone gives him the right to do so. Too many Christians don't know that they have the spiritual authority to fight their own battles—let alone help other believers fight theirs.

Another reason that people will turn to the dark side of the supernatural for help is because it looks easier and more effective than going to God for help. Satan can sell temporary "cures." Let's face it, coming to God for help requires something of us. We have to come to Him and open up our lives to Him. It can be painful and uncomfortable as we come face to face with who we are on the inside.

God cleanses and purifies, but the process is not a quick and easy cure. Thus, there is hardly ever just one exorcism in isolation. Usually it takes many exorcisms, along with therapy and inner healing, to bring spiritual wholeness. Over time, demonic strongholds get built into fortresses for the enemy to hide in, and it takes concerted effort to demolish those strongholds so as to get rid of the demons.

Temporary Cures and Allures

Why, then, do Satan's "cures" seem to work, at least for a while? A healer or medium can come and perform ceremonies over you or your house and it seems that things get better. As long as you don't dig below the surface, that is. The healer or medium does not require difficult soul-searching on your part. They temporarily smooth over your problem so that it doesn't bother you for a while. But then, because you have allowed the demons to have more legal room to wreak havoc, it resurges, compounded with interest. The deceptive calm does not last long. Oftentimes it is just when the person tries to go back to God, to attend church again, or start reading the Bible, that the demons kick up a new ruckus. It is far better to dig in and go to the root of the problems in your life instead of turning to the dark side of the supernatural for answers.

Instead of going to the occult, many turn to drugs and alcohol, which can also shackle them to the devil. When we were in Ukraine, we learned that thousands of addicts come through the Ukrainian Bible school's drug rehab program. We gave personal ministry to many recovered addicts during our stay in Ukraine. One night, as we were driving home, the driver inexplicably turned off on a side road. After bumping along for several miles, the car came to a stop at a compound. Since the driver didn't speak English, we had no way of knowing why we were there or what was going on.

Cautiously we exited the vehicle, stepping gingerly up to the front door. It swung open and to our immense relief, a Ukrainian friend stood there, and he understood English. He explained to us that we were at a very important drug rehab facility. He asked us if we would just take a few moments to pray with the people inside. Exhausted (a number of us had been fast asleep in the car), we agreed to come inside for a bit to pray with anyone who was still up. It was past midnight and as we drove it had seemed as if the whole country was in bed asleep. But as we walked through the halls of the rehab center, I was unprepared for what awaited me.

We were led into a small room that was packed full of people. Many were in pajamas, some even held children; all were there for help with rehabilitation. And all of them had stayed up for a blessing and a few minutes of prayer from us. Tess, Savannah, and I were surprised to see my dad getting all teary-eyed as he looked the room over. We wondered what we could possibly say to help assuage the pain that was so evident in everyone's eyes. We knew that we couldn't fix everything that night and we knew that most of the people in the room faced a long uphill battle to an addiction-free life. But they were trying. These men and women, young and old, now knew that it didn't work to dull their pain with substance abuse. All it had done was to give Satan more of a legal right to torment them.

It was a room full of pain. And tenuous hope. The people in the room had tried solving their problems with drugs and alcohol and other harmful substances, to no avail. Indulging in sin hadn't helped in any way, but now many were ready to try fixing their lives God's way. Now we were there, with a message of hope and deliverance. We spoke for a bit, encouraging and exhorting everyone in the room to not give up. We prayed for them as a whole and then decided to personally pray with and anoint everyone in the room. Tess, Savannah, Dad, and I each took some anointing oil and started working our way through the crowd.

It was a powerful time, because to the people gathered together that night, it was as if God was intervening personally for them. We didn't pray weak little prayers for them to feel good. We confronted the evil demons in their lives and ordered them to back off. We asked God to intervene and set these people free, not only from the drugs and alcohol, but from spiritual bondage as well. When an addict has a demon as well as a substance abuse problem, getting sober is especially difficult because the addict must fight with him- or herself as well as the demon who is trying to keep them shackled to their addiction.

The Eyes Have It

This was something new for these people. By themselves, they could not get victory over the demons because they didn't know how. Now we were joining them in taking a stand against the devil. (In ministry, I have often discovered that the devil and his demons need to be told to go, in so many words. I was working with a man one time and when I asked the demons why they were still there they said, "Well, no one has told us to go!")

That late night in Ukraine, we told those demons to go. As we prayed with people, we anointed them and then looked into their eyes. In some, I simply saw desperation and hope. In others, however, I saw evil looking back at me. I commanded Satan to loose them and to leave them alone.

In almost every interview I have ever been in, I have been asked about what I see when I look into a person's eyes. It's hard to describe. I don't think I can do it justice here, but I will try to explain. The eyes are the windows to the soul. Jesus put it this way: "The lamp of the body is the eye. If therefore your eye is good, your whole body will be full of light" (Matthew 6:22). The eyes are a reflection of what is inside you. Logically, if good can be seen in the eyes, evil can as well.

When I look a person in the eyes, sometimes I can catch a glimpse of the evil hiding out there. When that happens, it's like looking into the face of evil. The person might be a good person who loves the Lord, but a demon is not. When a demon manifests its presence, there's no mistaking the difference. When you look into the eyes of evil, it's not as though the person's eyes start glowing red, nor does the pupil enlarge to cover the whole eye. Spiritual discernment plays a large role in sensing a demon's presence. When I look into a demon-possessed person's eyes, I can see unadulterated hate. I can see the calculated coldness of evil. I can see a presence that would rip me limb from limb if it could. I see utter depravity. You can almost feel the evil presence in the air; it's as close to a glimpse of hell that you'll ever see. When you look into a person's eyes and a demon looks back at you, it's an intense stare. The first couple of times you see it, it can be really unnerving.

Sometimes I can look at a person and just know they have demons. It's as if the demon will take a peek at me from behind the person's eyes. This is not a kooky out-of-body sixth sense; it's more of a gut knowledge that something evil is looking at you. And so I look back. Because I have the Spirit of God in me, I can look right into that demon's eyes, knowing that it sees Jesus Christ shining in me. I don't have to be afraid for a moment. I can face that pure evil and cast it out because of God.

Any Christian can learn to exercise his or her heavenly authority over Satan and his demons. In the Bible school and in the drug rehab center, we showed people how to use their God-given authority to take their lives back from Satan. After we finished praying with and anointing everyone in the room, we then spent some time with the people who ran the rehab center.

Light Instead of Darkness

Sometimes people ask us why we let demons manifest and speak. It's because there is so much power in the spoken word. Just think, God created our entire world with just His words. All He had to say was, "Let there be light!" and light came into existence. Likewise, with our words we can invite a demon in—or cast it out. And when you use your God-given authority over the dark side of the supernatural to cast out a demon, causing the demon to renounce its right to remain in you or another person, then it must leave, because it is bound by its word.

Those of us who deal with deliverance often know how it works. Not so for most American pastors and church leaders. For the most part, they are uncomfortable about interacting with demons, and their authority has eroded over time. They don't want to take a controversial stand, and they don't like to take risks.

Sadly, many in this generation have looked over their pastors, priests, and spiritual leaders and decided that their words mean next to nothing anymore. Many teenagers nowadays have no real moral guidance, not even from their parents. Some of us have been blessed to grow up in Christian homes where we learn about morality and the difference between right and wrong, good and evil. But just the same, the church and its pastors hold very little sway over today's youth, who are more influenced by evil and immorality as a result. Across the board, only 20 percent of Americans regularly attend church, and even fewer teenagers and young adults.

I hope you know that when you grow up not having learned the difference between right and wrong, you can become easy pickings for Satan and his cronies. America is becoming a spiritual vacuum, with no real strong church leadership for the young people of America. Living in a generation that has a poorly defined spiritual, moral, and theological viewpoint means that a whole generation has lost its perspective. So who will step in and fill the hole left by people of integrity and morality? What does the younger generation look to for some sort of moral compass and example? The entertainment industry, singers, sports figures, actors, and celebrities. What a terrifying fact! For guidance, students and teenagers are looking to people who are just as messed up as they are. Oprah is revered for her spirituality and insight; Beyonce is a role model for young women; Chris Brown beats up his girlfriends and is still making millions. These are the role models of today?

With zero spiritual convictions, the only ethic that guides this generation is called "do it if it feels good." When Lady Gaga sings about making love to Judas, young people don't see it as a spiritual issue. "It's just a song." Pastors and godly men and women, have taken a backseat to clueless celebrities. Entertainment has changed from being an occasional pastime to something that is all-absorbing and socially acceptable. "Edgy" is cool. The pervasiveness of evil escapes most teenagers because the whole society has become largely desensitized to it. Even my youngest sister has been exposed to things that I didn't have to deal with until I was twice as old as she is. The devil, quite frankly, is having a field day. And the degradation of American morality shows no signs of slowing.

In this kind of an environment, people who are in pain and need of help go wherever they can to find it. Without ethical or moral anchors, they seek help from darkness by looking at it. But there is no relief from darkness and confusion on the dark side of the supernatural, only deeper darkness and toxic confusion.

We are trying to do something about this self-defeating mindset. We are putting the darkness on notice: God's light is shining!

CHAPTER 7

Not Just a Harmless Movie

A crusading Christian with a cross I am not. I don't render unto the fire every evil book and piece of occult paraphernalia that I come across. To do so would take up all of my time. And the real problem, the social mindset, would be unaltered. I am aware that the prevailing viewpoint of the world I live in has morphed into a culture of "anything goes." In this postmodern, relativistic society, to take a moral stance on anything is a death knell to the all-compelling "cool factor."

Paradoxically, this anything-goes culture is riddled with taboo subjects. Mention a touchy subject and you will offend someone. People are especially sensitive to religious matters. To voice "religious" objections to popular forms of entertainment is one of the surest ways to get someone's defenses up; moral or religious concerns will never get a fair hearing.

To the reader who may love some of the materials I am about call out, please hear me. Understand that while I write from a perspective of someone who has a deep understanding of the reality of spiritual warfare, I am also writing from the perspective of a teenager who enjoys a good book or movie as much as anyone. I understand the almost magnetic pull of *The Walking Dead* and *Harry Potter*. Yes, these masterful creative epics are vastly entertaining, but there is a very real spiritual side to these works as well, and it must not be ignored. To do so may grant the enemy squatter's rights to encroach on your spiritual freedom more than you bargained for. The war is not lost in a single great battle, but in a series of concessions that can lead to one's downfall. I urge you to be vigilant and aware, not to be led astray by fancy rhetoric or entertaining sideshows.

Satan is a wily entity. I am not being paranoid, and I know that God is by far the greater one. But the devil is much craftier and more clever than you or I, and he knows us better than we know ourselves. He knows perfectly well how to exploit our every weakness.

Today's media-induced haze provides Satan with plenty of opportunity. The average adult spends nearly eleven hours a day using some form of mass media for information and entertainment. It comes in a constant stream. None of the books, movies, and TV shows is mindless entertainment. There is an underlying message that sticks in our brains and stays with us, influencing our thoughts and actions.

If the devil were to orchestrate something so out-front and evil that it was unmistakable, many people would refuse to participate. So he uses stealth. He infiltrates every form of entertainment and information-broadcasting out there, gradually. I want to take a look at a selection of popular movies, books and TV shows to illustrate just how far Satan has pushed into the popular mind. Even if you disagree with me, please hear me out and consider the information I am about to present before you make an informed decision that you can stand by.

While I recognize that these movies and TV shows which I use for examples may soon fade away, the principles and ideas will not. Look beyond the title and characters to see the underlying message that I am addressing. Remember my years of witnessing firsthand just how far the devil can push someone before they wake up to find their life in shambles. Like the song that you can't get out of your head or the movie you've seen countless times, you can come to accept and believe things that are beyond the pale, and your friends and family may be right alongside you, having also bought into the lies.

Harry Potter: Boy Witch

It's not just a harmless book or movie series. The Harry Potter franchise has ignited contention among people of every religious background since the first book was published in 1997. The fanciful stories of a young boy wizard, the books have been touted as magnificent writing achievements that draw in young and old readers. School-teachers use these books to motivate reluctant readers, and many extoll the morals showcased in the books. Classes centered on the mystique of Harry Potter have sprung up all over the world for all ages, in kindergartens and honors colleges. Discussed everywhere from casual sleepovers to highbrow literary circles, the series has sold over 500 million copies, cementing it at the top of the heap. *Harry Potter* is the best-selling book series of all time.

But is *Harry Potter* really just an innocuous book that encourages children to read? What happens when one looks at it from a biblical and a spiritual perspective? The story chronicles an orphan boy named Harry on his adventures as he seeks to avenge his parent's deaths and defeat evil magic and sorcery with "good" magic. He discovers that he is a wizard or witch and that his parents were also powerful witches. He is taken to Hogwart's School of Wizardry and Witchcraft to hone his skills as a witch.

Readers delve into the story as Harry learns about all manner of supernatural and occult phenomena: divination, sorcery, the study of ancient runes, the history of magic, defense against the dark arts, alchemy, charms, ghouls, and xylomancy (a form of divination with twigs). At one point in the story, Harry is forced to enter into a blood covenant though the shedding of his own blood. The witches in these stories have god-like powers, with the ability to usurp the free will of others and to take life. Harry sports a permanent scar of a lightning bolt on his forehead, which is an historic symbol of satanic worship. I have met many people who have tattoos of this lightning bolt on their foreheads and other parts of their bodies. That shows how much people adore the series.

From a Biblical Perspective

Before I weigh in on the Harry Potter craze, let's examine other books and movies under the light of God's Word. I want to broaden the scope to include other witchcraft-themed entertainment such as the TV show, *Supernatural*, or the movie, *Beautiful Creatures*.

Every word of the Old and New Testaments is God-inspired. Starting from the beginning of recorded history, God has been warning His people of the dangers of witch-craft and divination. One of the best examples is when He delivered His people out of Egypt in the Great Exodus, setting apart the Israelites as His people and giving them a new way to live. He established His laws and command-ments and warned His people what would happen should they stray. For instance, God commands the Israelites:

When you come into the land which the Lord your God is giving you, you shall not learn to follow the abominations of those nations. There shall not be found among you anyone who makes his son or his daughter pass through the fire [child sacrifice], *or one who practices witchcraft, or a soothsayer, or one who interprets omens, or a sorcerer, or one who conjures spells, or a medium, or a spiritist, or one who calls up the dead. For all who do these things are an abomination to the Lord, and because of these abominations the Lord your God drives them out from before you.* (Deuteronomy 18:9–12)

In particular, God made two things very clear. First, He is very specific in naming different forms of witchcraft. God wanted no ambiguity. It is clear that He loathes witchcraft. God deplores many sins in the Bible, but few are labeled as "an abomination" to Him. That's pretty strong language. An abomination is something so loathsome and disgusting and hateful that it cannot be tolerated. Second, God wasn't just giving the Israelites empty land; the people who had lived there before them were driven out by God because of their evil practices. Let that sink in. With all the evil and sin that the people of every nation committed, these nations were so evil and full of witchcraft that God drove them out. And He certainly did not want His people to follow in their predecessors' evil footsteps. He brought them into the Promised Land because He wanted to have a holy people who were set apart to Him.

Later, God warned again, "Give no regard to mediums and familiar spirits; do not seek after them, to be defiled by them: I am the Lord your God" (Leviticus 19:31). Throughout the Old Testament, the penalty for witchcraft was death. Clearly, God did not take witchcraft and sorcery lightly. A person was committing a serious offense to have anything to do with witchcraft. King Saul, the first king of the Israelites, lost both his kingdom and his life when he went to visit the Witch of Endor.

The New Testament also condemns witchcraft many times. For example, Paul wrote:

> *Now the works of the flesh are evident, which are: adultery, fornication, uncleanness, lewdness, idolatry, **sorcery**, hatred, contentions, jealousies, outbursts of wrath, selfish ambitions, dissensions, heresies, envy, murders, drunkenness, revelries, and the like; of which I tell you beforehand, just as I also told you in time past, that those who practice such things will not inherit the kingdom of God.* (Galatians 5:19–21, emphasis mine)

One of the reasons God has such a loathing for sorcery is because it represents outright spiritual rebellion: "For rebellion is as the sin of witchcraft, and stubbornness is as iniquity and idolatry…" (1 Samuel 15:23). Witchcraft uses supernatural powers outside of God's limits. Practicing witchcraft circumvents God's rules and laws to try and gain power to accomplish things without God. Whether they know it or not, witches, receive their powers from Satan, who is a sworn enemy of God. God does not take kindly to rebellion. Even entertaining it makes a bystander just as guilty as the witch.

So God has painted a pretty clear picture: witchcraft is a complete no-no. There is no "good magic" to counterbalance "bad magic." It is all bad, and God condemns it. He condemns the practice of and participation in sorcery and witchcraft. He abhors the consultation of witches or spiritists. If God is dead set against it, why do we go near the stuff? Why do we see Sunday schools with Harry Potter-themed vacation Bible schools?

From An Exorcist's Perspective

You have probably already figured out where I fall on the Harry Potter spectrum. There's a lot that I don't agree with in the books and movies, but I am just going to point out a couple of really big, gaping faults that Harry Potter has. Pope Benedict XVI put it very succinctly when he said, "It is good that you shed light and information on the Harry Potter matter, for these are subtle seductions that are barely noticeable and precisely because of that deeply affect [children] and corrupt the Christian faith in souls even before it [the faith] could properly grow and mature." He understands how insidious something like the *Harry Potter* series can be to a Christian's faith.

I'm sure I could come up with many more, but here are just a few concerns I have about the Harry Potter books. These concerns aren't unique to the *Harry Potter* series; many popular books and movies carry the same themes of witchcraft and evil. The books and movies promote a worldview that is condemned by God. God has forbidden witchcraft. It is an insidious evil in all forms and must be avoided. We become desensitized to the evil practices that we read about or view on the screen. The shock of evil is dulled and more concessions are made as a result.

Stories like *Harry Potter* and *Supernatural* endorse the enormous lie that there is "good" magic. Harry fights black magic with white magic. The trouble with that is that there is no such thing as "good magic." *All* witches derive their powers from one place: the devil. This is probably one of the most dangerous ideas presented in the book, namely that it is OK to use magic as long as it's for good purposes.

What defines a "good purpose," anyway? People seek out occult power in order to obtain revenge. Harry uses his powers to avenge his parents' death.

Without a doubt, such books and movies glamorize witchcraft, disobedience, and magic. People become desensitized to the evil of witchcraft and supernatural occurrences as they are relegated to the harmless world of make-believe. The popularity of *Harry Potter* has caused a huge increase of interest in the occult and witchcraft, and the market for witchcraft-related items has exploded.

In spite of God's prohibition of witchcraft, almost all of my friends have read the *Harry Potter* series and viewed the movies, and most of them will vehemently defend it. Some of my best friends are fans of the hit TV show *Supernatural*, in which two brothers battle the "forces of evil" with even more wickedness than Harry Potter. The brothers, Sam and Dean, hold séances frequently, in which they elaborately summon demons. Witchcraft and sorcery is practiced by "the good guys," and one of the brothers even has sexual intercourse with a demon.

My friends who are *Supernatural* fans are Christians and they know the Bible. Yet they blithely indulge in entertainment that consists of witchcraft, sorcery, and magic. I think the connection between biblical knowledge and application has been lost somewhere. Many genuinely think that as long as they don't "believe" in what they are watching then they are OK. That's simply a lame excuse for doing whatever you want and watching whatever you want. Come on, guys, really! Think this through. Do you honestly think that being a part of this whole Harry Potter craze is pleasing to God? God hates evil. It's as simple as that. Remember that there are thousands of other worthwhile books and movies in the world. Just go read something else that doesn't compromise your spiritual integrity!

Three Reasons Witches are Wild about Harry Potter

Real witches all over the world couldn't be happier with everyone's obsession with Harry Potter and the supernatural.

In fact, when my father recently visited London on a ministry trip, he decided to tour for a day. He stopped by Shakespeare's house in Stratford, and as he was leaving, he noticed a nearby witchcraft shop. He ducked in for a moment. Standing in the front of the store was a cardboard cutout of everyone's favorite boy witch, Harry. A large portion of the store was taken up with Harry Potter paraphernalia. The store was full of books, wands, spell books, wizard's hats, and even broomsticks. Dad stopped and talked with a clerk and asked what he thought of the Harry Potter craze. The witch said, "Oh! We love Harry Potter! It's the best thing that's ever happened to us! Business is booming, and people are really getting interested in what we do." Witches are getting a good deal with this global glamorization and acceptance of witchcraft. I can think of three more three reasons why witches are wild about all of the good press they are getting: (1) It compliments their public relations campaign for acceptance, (2) it teaches kids to not be afraid of the powers of witchcraft, and (3) it makes witchcraft seem kid-friendly.

What About Demons?

Can you get demons from reading or watching *Harry Potter* and the like? Yes and no. Every person has a different and unique response. For some people, playing with an Ouija board or reading *Harry Potter* is enough to open the door to the devil. But I have talked with other people who have done all sorts of things that I would expect to allow demons in, and somehow they got off demon-free.

A better question to ask is: Is it worth the risk? Do you really want to find out if reading *Harry Potter* or watching *Supernatural* will allow demons to infest your life or start you down a path to a deeper involvement in the occult? I sure don't! When it comes to spiritual warfare, I have learned that the more right you are with God and the less sin you have in your life, the more powerful you are against the enemy and the dark side of the supernatural.

Every time a Christian does something to compromise his or her spiritual integrity even a little, it undermines spiritual authority over the devil and his demons. Actively engaging in something that glorifies evil is dangerous to the soul. Even watching or reading something "just for entertainment" does not make it safe.

Here's another way to look at the issue: My university is a "dry" campus, meaning that the consumption of alcohol is not allowed and doing so can get you kicked off campus. Not only are we not allowed to drink, but we are not allowed to even be around people who are imbibing spirits, because that makes us guilty by association. It's the same with witchcraft. Even though you may not be the one casting the spells, you are still guilty of opening yourself up to the occult and supernatural by the books you read. At my school, it is against the rules to even be around alcohol. In God's Kingdom, it is against the rules to be around witchcraft and the occult.

The best way to steer clear of demons is to live by the words of Philippians 4:8—"Finally, brethren, whatever things are true, whatever things are noble, whatever things are just, whatever things are pure, whatever things are lovely, whatever things are of good report, if there is any virtue and if there is anything praiseworthy—meditate on these things." I hardly think books and movies like *Harry Potter* and *Twilight* (a book and movie series that glorifies vampirism) would fit into any of those categories. With all of the excellent books and movies that have been and are being produced, why waste time on questionable drivel? If you are going to continue watching and reading things that God frowns upon, at least have the integrity to admit what you are doing instead of covering up your sin with polite excuses. Don't lie to yourself. Joseph Goebbels, Hitler's propaganda minister, once said, "If you repeat a lie often enough, people will believe it, and you will even come to believe it yourself."

Occult and supernatural subject matter has wormed its way into popular books, movies and TV shows. Stay away from it, unless you are researching the subject matter or apologetically responding to it. Even then, be careful, lest you leave yourself more open to the devil than you realize.

CHAPTER 8

Interesting Faces
of the Supernatural

Ghosts, goblins, vampires, shapeshifters, werewolves, and demons. Under various names, these otherworldly apparitions have haunted humanity from the beginnings of civilization. We see them in the ancient Minoan and Canaanite cultures. We see evidence of them in the history of the people on every continent. Standing in checkout lines, we read the headlines about UFO sightings along with the latest gossip about a celebrity's spiritual interests. Countless people vow they have had ghost sightings and paranormal experiences. Popular TV shows a few years ago featured ghost-hunters chasing and documenting alleged sightings filmed with spooky night-vision goggles. People talk about participating in séances to communicate with the dead. Is all of this attention to supernatural activity driven merely by marketing or a desire for fifteen minutes of fame? Is it fictitious, or is there some truth to the many reports of contact with the "other side"?

When it comes to the supernatural, even people without godly faith sense that there are good and evil forces. Many believe that God represents the good, yet they have no distinction or explanation for whom or what controls the bad. Christians who read their Bibles know that the actual puppeteer behind the many masks of the dark side is the great deceiver, Satan. He is crafty and knows that evil in its purest and most obvious form (such as a demon) would be shunned by most people, so he creatively dresses up his evil.

The supernatural has only two sides, good light and bad dark, and one side cleverly covers up his truly evil form. Let me state it a different way: All supernatural occurrences stem only from these two sources—God and the devil. Jesus said "He who is not with Me is against Me," (Matthew 12:30). This is pretty clear. These creatures of the dark side that I will be addressing are just a few examples of the creatively evil lures with which the devil goes fishing for human beings. It represents the side where evil and fear reign.

Good Versus Evil

It's not only Christians who view supernatural things this way. Many religions and cults, as well as social scientists, agree that two main supernatural powers are contending with each other. Christians believe God with His glory is the strongest one, and yet the other side, Satan, diametrically opposed to the true and good God, is a force to be reckoned with. Since almost the beginning of time, a battle has been raging between good and evil, light and darkness. Ever since God cast the rebellious Lucifer (aka Satan) out of Heaven, he has been in constant opposition against God. His goal has been to kill, steal, and destroy anything that God loves. And God's greatest love is humanity. So Satan has come after us with the full force of all of his power and demons, trying to drag us away from God.

Satan isn't simply an impersonal evil force that is out to terrorize others. He used to be God's brightest angel, clever and beautiful. He is an entity who is much smarter and more powerful than any measly human. He is a cunning enemy, the most deadly enemy you will ever face. Look to the ancient priests of Egypt to get just an idea of how powerful the devil really is. When Moses came before Pharaoh and turned his staff into a snake by God's power, the Egyptian black magic priests were able to do that as well! They were also able to turn water into blood and perform other unbelievable feats. They received their power directly from the devil.

You may ask, "Well, if the devil's such a bad guy, why wasn't humanity wiped out long ago?" God is the reason why. He alone holds Satan at bay. It is through His power that Christians can cast out demons. Satan has to play by the rules. It seems odd, doesn't it, that the master of all evil has rules and laws that he cannot break. No matter how powerful and evil the devil is, he has to obey the rules and laws that are laid down and enforced by God. Satan can't harm a child of God unless individuals allow or open doors to give him that right. That right is what we call the legal right; it is some legitimate reason that allows Satan to interfere in your life.

Apart from some sin that opens the door to the enemy, we carry on with life in a state of protected human innocence. We live under what is called the "common grace" of God. It covers all of us, believer and unbeliever alike. Think of an umbrella. As long as you don't do anything to grant Satan a legal right, you are safe under the umbrella of God's protection and Satan can't harm you. But if you do something that God has forbidden, you step out from under that umbrella. Essentially, you voluntarily grant the devil the right to attack you. Of course Satan's goal is to get you to do just that. And he's become very skilled at presenting his temptations.

For many people, dark-side topics such as ghosts, vampires, witchcraft, or necromancy are very attractive. They don't understand that all of the dark side of the supernatural is a ploy to circumvent the common grace of God in order to create a legal right to attack.

Ghosts and Hauntings

"Ghosts" have played their haunting tricks with people, places, and things since ancient times. Even today, twenty-first-century Americans report ghost sightings, and they certainly flock to see the latest ghostbuster-themed shows and movies.

Thought to be the souls or spirits of departed people or even pets, ghosts are believed to haunt places or people that they associated with in life. Sightings range from vague, wispy shapes to eerily lifelike facsimiles to departed loved ones. Occasionally, people claim to have been touched physically by these beings. Millions of dollars have been spent either to rid haunted houses of spirits or to summon the ghosts and communicate with them.

Even as an exorcist, the idea of encountering a ghostly vision gives me the chills. It is disconcerting and yet strangely fascinating. The idea of being able to communicate with the dead seems inviting sometimes, and it's not a new one. But ghosts are *not* dearly departed souls. They are demons in disguise.

In other words, there are no such things as ghosts. But there are demons who masquerade as ghosts, and that's even more dangerous. If a "ghost" can get you so worked up that you call your local witch or spiritist healer to cleanse you or your house, the devil's got you. Worse yet, if you try to communicate with the ghost of grandpa or grandma, you are committing necromancy, a practice forbidden by God. And the devil's got you there as well.

Remember, there are no redeeming qualities about a demon. A demon is pure evil. If you are being visited by ghosts, you need to get help. Be careful who you go to. Many people will claim that they can help. Some may lay claim to the title "Christian." But more often than not they bring in more demons than they get rid of. There is no middle ground here. No matter how convincing the ghost is, it is a *demon!*

The Bible has a lot to say about life after death. Never does it mention disembodied souls wandering the earth. Hebrews 9:27 tells us how death and the afterlife really works: "[I]t is appointed for men to die once, but after this the judgment." God doesn't send ghosts to people, and if something is not of God, it is of the devil.

As an exorcist, you get to hear crazy ghost stories. My father has been to countless haunted houses and experienced some frightening things. People have told me stories of hearing doors opening and closing, strange knocking sounds, lights and TVs going off and on. Shadows and shapes appear out of nowhere. I have heard stories of people leaving a room and coming back minutes later to find the room torn to bits. I have heard of people being thrown against walls by an unseen force and appearances of shadowy people. I have no doubt that many have experienced these types of things. But ghosts were not involved; demons were. The people are unaware of the true source of these occurrences.

My father told me of once meeting with a family who believed that they had demons. He arrived at their quaint little house and sat down in the living room with them all. He started talking to the mother about her problems. Off-handedly, she mentioned that recently she was visited by her grandmother. Dad paid no thought to this until the lady added later that her grandma had been dead for five years. Upon closer questioning, the lady revealed that quite frequently the ghost of grandma came to visit her. She spoke with fondness of the visits, saying how pleased she was to be able to talk with her loving grandma again. As she was talking, she paused suddenly and looking over dad's shoulder said "Oh! There she is right there behind you. Do you see her?" Dad turned and looked, but didn't see anyone. However, knowing the true nature of "grandma" he prayed "God, I ask you to reveal to this woman the demon behind this 'grandma.'"

Suddenly the woman's face contorted into a look of horror, and she shrieked in terror. She curled up on the floor screaming for the demon to get away from her. Dad prayed with her and gradually she calmed down. God had shown her the ugliness hiding behind the "ghost" and the lady wanted no part in it.

Get it straight: Ghosts aren't cute little mischief-making visitors. They are really disguised demons and they need to be confronted as such. While some may seem benign at first, things usually go bad quickly and more often than not people come to us terrified of the violent hauntings in their homes. There is nothing friendly or harmless about these familiar visitors.

Vampires

Edward Cullen, vampire star of the *Twilight* series, is not going to be showing up on your doorstep anytime soon. Nor will any of his buddies. Vampires are a product of medieval folklore, the "undead," reanimated corpses who feast on blood. These fearful creatures were reputed to rise from the grave at night to suck their victims dry of their life's blood. They once inspired revulsion and horror. Now, though, they star in hit TV shows, books, and movies. How has such a repulsive creature been turned into something powerful (although dark) and seductive? Vampires have been romanticized, and this has opened up a dangerous door to the occult that many teenagers are walking through unknowingly.

So vampires aren't real. But this fascination with them is just as dangerous. People are obsessed not just with the idea of vampires' existence, but with the concept that they can become a vampire too. And that's where they walk on spiritual quicksand.

Before I share my experiences with the vampirism trend, let's look at it from a biblical perspective. First, let's be honest with ourselves about their evil nature. Vampires are reanimated corpses. They are killers; their victims die from their "attentions." They drink blood, which is detestable to God. They are somehow immortal, which also violates God's plan for humanity. Their drinking of human blood perverts the atoning blood of Christ's sacrifice on the cross. But there is no redeeming quality whatsoever to a vampire (or to someone who is trying to be like one). All these creatures have going for them is some kind of sex appeal, and even that is tenuous. We have to believe that people aren't trying to emulate vampires because of their upstanding citizenship!

Needless to say, there simply isn't room in the Bible for God to address every specific thing that people may choose to do. There wouldn't be enough pages in the world for that! Instead, God gave us principles, ways of living that are enough to direct us to make the right decisions. So while God may not have a chapter titled "Thou shalt not try to be like vampires," we still know that God frowns upon vampirism. In the Old Testament, when God was giving commands to His people on how to live, He instructed as follows:

"And whatever man of the house of Israel, or of the strangers who dwell among you, who eats any blood, I will set My face against that person who eats blood, and will cut him off from among his people. For the life of the flesh is in the blood, and I have given it to you upon the altar to make atonement for your souls; for it is the blood that makes atonement for the soul." Therefore I said to the children of Israel, "No one among you shall eat blood, nor shall any stranger who dwells among you eat blood."

"Whatever man of the children of Israel, or of the strangers who dwell among you, who hunts and catches any animal or bird that may be eaten, he shall pour out its blood and cover it with dust; for it is the life of all flesh. Its blood sustains its life." Therefore I said to the children of Israel, "You shall not eat the blood of any flesh, for the life of all flesh is its blood. Whoever eats it shall be cut off."
(Leviticus 17:10–14)

God wasn't kidding around. Not only was human blood to remain untouched, except for medical reasons, but animal blood as well was to be poured out on the ground and covered. God gave these commands because the life is in the blood. Before Christ came and died on a cross to make atonement for our sins, atonement for sins occurred through the death of an animal, in a religious sacrifice. It was through the blood. That is why, when Christ died on the cross for our sins, it was through the shedding of His blood that we could be forgiven. Without the shedding of this life-blood, we would all perish for our sins.

Vampirism perverts this grace by advocating the drinking of something that was never meant to be drunk. God considers it a sin to drink blood, and the penalty was pretty stiff for doing it. If you were caught, you would be cut off from your people. You would have to forfeit your family, your possessions, and your life as an Israelite. That's a very high cost.

Even much later, after Christ's death and ascension up to heaven, it was still important to God. Luke wrote to the people in the early church:

> *For it seemed good to the Holy Spirit, and to us, to lay upon you no greater burden than these necessary things: that you abstain from things offered to idols, from blood, from things strangled, and from sexual immorality. If you keep yourselves from these, you will do well.* (Acts 15:28–29).

Note that Luke likened the sin of drinking blood to sexual immorality! Transgressing in this way provides an open door, a legal right, for Satan to take advantage of.

Obviously there aren't demons disguised as vampires walking the earth drinking blood. The devil is much too clever for that. Instead, he has turned humans into walking vampire-wannabes! This is the danger I see that comes with a fascination in vampires and vampirism. By drinking blood, or entering into a blood covenant, you grant Satan a right to come into your life. You open yourself up for demonic possession. Shockingly, that's just what thousands of teens are doing. With this vampire craze, many have acted out being a vampire. The stories I have heard would horrify you. I have worked with teen girls who have done crazy things in the name of vampires. They have put blood in their boyfriend's food. And they cut themselves in order to drink their own blood. Little girls play vampires and take turns biting each other's necks. A couple in England, who are self-styled vampires, cut themselves and drink each other's blood regularly! Satanism of course has rituals and ceremonies involving blood. All of this is sick and perverted.

In all of the exorcisms I have done, there is great significance in the power of blood. I have lost track of how many times I have worked with someone who has had a demon because either they or an ancestor made a "blood covenant" by means of which their family line was cursed and demons were granted legal rights.

Remember, by the shedding of Christ's blood He redeemed from death all who believe in Him. It is just as easy to be set free by blood as it is to be bound by it. My advice: Stay away from anything that perverts the meaning of blood. Blood is a good thing, it keeps us alive and by the shedding of innocent blood we were all saved from the condemnation of death. However, Satan has again perverted something wonderful that comes from God. Avoid the drinking of blood and entering into blood covenants; it is sin, plain and simple. Don't give Satan that legal right over your life. If you already have, turn to God with all your heart and ask Him to lead you out of bondage.

Shapeshifters and Werewolves

Like vampires, shapeshifters and werewolves are now immensely popular in romance novels. The idea of creatures that are half-human and half-beast traces its roots to the cradle of civilization. The biblical Nephilim, who were half-human and half-demon, the ancient Babylonian gods, the Egyptian gods, the Greek and Roman gods, the ancient Nordic gods, and even mermaids are examples of the notion of human hybridization and shapeshifting.

Shapeshifters, along with werewolves (also known as lycanthropes) obviously do not exist in the real world. However, there are several aspects about them that can have a negative impact on us, whether they are make-believe or not.

Let's examine shapeshifters first. Researching for this book, I did some Internet searches on the topic and found some troubling results. Thousands of romance books have been written—about the erotic love between a shapeshifter and his or her human lover. Most of the books are relatively new, and it seems as if today's culture is making a broad circle-back to ancient beliefs. This goes along with the recent upsurge of interest in the supernatural and paranormal. However, these fictional beings—werewolves, vampires, and shapeshifters of all kinds—are nothing new.

Shapeshifting has a colorful history. The word is only loosely defined, meaning the ability to physically transform into different forms. This is usually seen in human-to-animal transformations. In Greek mythology, we can read tales of their gods shifting into animal forms to mate and interact with humans. Stories like the ones about Leda and the Swan and Europa being captured and raped by the god Zeus in the form of a bull may be mythological, but they portray bestiality and sick debauchery.

In His Law, God commanded: "Nor shall you mate with any animal, to defile yourself with it. Nor shall any woman stand before an animal to mate with it. It is perversion" (Leviticus 18:23). The penalty for bestiality was death. And yet, in other cultures, such perversion was normal. Look at the Egyptians and Sumerians. Once again, we see that bestiality was common and in some religions was used as a way to worship gods.

Today's modern shapeshifting romances at best border on bestiality, if not dangerously portraying it outright. A warning from an exorcist: Participating in that kind of sin *will* get you demons. Don't read those books!

The shapeshifter fantasy has a spiritual component as well. There are many animalistic demons. I have seen them manifest in people with my own eyes. There are serpent demons, as well as bear, lion, wolf, eagle, dog, and cat demons. It's not uncommon for a person to hiss like a snake or bark like a dog when they have an animal spirit. There are several ways to acquire animal-like demons. One of most common ways is by looking for animal spirit guides, trying to build a spiritual connection to an animal. What people don't know is that they are not connecting with animals, they are connecting with demons.

While the idea of changing back and forth from human existence to subhuman life forms is an ancient one, it is still very much alive today on the dark side of the supernatural. There are very dark and powerful witch doctors and shamans who claim to be able to shift into animals. While it might sound crazy, there have been hundreds of reports and stories of such things, and in our ministry, we have heard eyewitness accounts. I do think it is possible for a person to shapeshift into another form, but it requires dark, unimaginably evil power to do so. As I mentioned earlier, we know that by using black magic, the ancient Egyptians were able to replicate some of God's miracles. When Moses went before Pharaoh to demand that he release God's people, God told Moses to give them a sign. So Moses put his staff forward and God changed it into a snake. Seems impossible right? That's what everyone must have been thinking, when suddenly, Pharaoh's high priests were able to do the same thing! Through Satan's power, they changed a wooden stick into a living snake. God triumphed in the end however, and Moses's snake ate the other two priests' snakes.

This is just one example of how powerful Satan really is. One of the most dangerous things a Christian can do is to underestimate him. In the book of Revelation, which details the end of time, the antichrist will perform miracles through the power of Satan. Beware of shapeshifting, unless you want to play with actual demonic possession.

Much of what I have said applies to werewolves as well. Werewolves are half-human half-wolf beasts who stay in human form during the day but turn into murdering wolves at night. The idea of half-human hybrids is not a new one. Here is the dangerous concept that lurks behind all of these illusions: by making a human half-animal, morality is tossed to the wayside. Animals aren't moral. They have no compunction about right or wrong. Most vampire, werewolf, and shapeshifter novels are based on that idea. The "creature" kills, and it is OK, because they have no morality or ethic code to live by. When a vampire or werewolf decides to kill or not to kill, it is merely a decision, nothing more. The idea of humans being created in the divine image of God is thrown aside in favor of animalistic instincts. God created animals, too, but He set distinct boundaries between them and human men and women, whom He created in His image. To blend the two is a violation of divine law. Even to play around with the idea puts you on a very dangerous path.

From the werewolf romance novels that I have seen on the market (there are thousands of them) I see a strong possibility of stumbling into bestiality. No man or woman should desire to have sex with animals, but werewolves and shapeshifters blur those moral lines. Here is the bottom line: God made humans and He made animals. Humans have been given authority *over* animals, because we bear God's divine image. Humans aren't meant to *be* animals. Humans have a conscience and we have the power of reason. We must live by a moral code, accountable to God.

A common demon that I have run into is a demon called Loki. The name comes from the old Norse gods and it means "trickster." I'm not talking about the charmingly suave Loki portrayed by the Marvel comics. The real Loki is revoltingly evil. In Norse mythology he would take on animal forms to have intercourse with animals and gods. One of the forms that he would take was that of a wolf. When I run into demons named Loki, they bear his characteristics and sometimes even act like a wolf.

Satan has been able to use this fascination with shape-shifting and werewolves to gain a legal right to torment God's people. He has many ways of perverting divine and natural order. God made us human, not animal. So what's wrong with watching a vampire or werewolf movie or reading a shapeshifter romance novel? Will that get you demons? In and of itself, probably not, but there is a very real danger cloaked behind all of this fantasy. By hybridizing humans, something foundational to human identity gets bypassed: morality. It is all too easy to slip into thinking that living out of instincts, irresponsibly, is just as good as living in obedience to the moral principles of God and under His grace. Satan will do anything that he can to undermine and chip away at God's truth and at civilized behavior. It's all a part of his bigger plan to corrupt human thinking and to dehumanize and devalue the miracle of human life.

Pop Culture Fad or Paradigm Shift?

What's really going on here? Am I over-reacting to just another pop culture fascination that will fade in time? Since most of this is fantasy anyway, why be too troubled by it? Every generation gets into weird stuff and this is just the latest. Or is it? Is my generation experiencing a paradigm consciousness shift in how the supernatural and spiritual reality are viewed? Are we entering into a no-rules, post-biblical age when the most basic of moral boundaries no longer exist? Is it possible that we are truly nearing the return of Christ, and that we are experiencing again what it was like "in the days of Noah," as Jesus warned us in Luke 17:26? It was the Flood the first time, but it will be the fire next time.

Even if this current fad fades, the sinister trends I've described in this chapter should make you think seriously about how far you yourself may have stepped over a line by indulging in an interest in such things, even for "just entertainment." Think again before you do it or allow others to forsake their moral compass. Remember God's moral absolutes. Do not ignore His boundaries for the sake of hearing a werewolf's howl of terror or vicariously contemplating a vampire's bite. Satan, you know, is the ultimate shapeshifter: "Satan himself transforms himself into an angel of light" (2 Corinthians 11:14).

CHAPTER 9

From C.S. Lewis to Harry Potter

If you didn't know any better, the shop looked charming and welcoming. It was nestled in a picturesque alley in the bustling city of London, England, in one of the busiest tourist sections of the city. It was one of the most famous new age and witchcraft shops in the area, and business was booming. Enter the Teenage Exorcists. Tess, Savannah, my Dad, and I were on a tour in London. The BBC, which had filmed us at home and followed us to Ukraine, had brought the three of us to London for the final chapter on the documentary that they were filming. They wanted to film us interacting with witches and others who didn't share our belief that what they did was evil. A bit unsure of what we would find, the three of us walked into the store with a feeling of trepidation.

This was one of the first times that I had been in such an occult store. It was creatively decorated and had the sweet, cloying smell of burning incense. It was open and light, hardly living up to the stereotypical witchcraft store. The proprietress was warm and accommodating as she gave us a tour of her shop. There was so much to take in! We didn't know where to look first. So we wandered around, examining the occult paraphernalia it housed.

Near the front were bins of different rocks. I recognized them as aura rocks. Some had stickers that claimed to heal; others claimed to give peace and serenity. They were quite pretty, and the witch who ran the shop tried to get me to pick one up. I refused of course, because these rocks had had all sorts of incantations and curses spoken over them. To pick one up and accept it would be to allow whatever had been prayed over the rock to take root in my life. And it would not be warm happy thoughts and feelings, either.

We moved on to the back of the room where there was a large Native American display.

There were kachina dolls, Indian headdresses, and dream catchers along with a book of Indian incantations. Clustered around were books on spirit guides and "soul awakening" CDs. Here and there throughout the displays, the odd incense stick was burning. In the back room an entire supply closet had been turned into a mini garden with shrines to ancestors and miniature Buddhas cluttering the diminutive landscaping. There were erotic and sensual

New Age books scattered everywhere as well as several editions of the sexually explicit Hindu Kama Sutra.

Back in the front of the store, amidst the tarot cards and crystals, was a full display case of Harry-Potter-worthy wands. As the other girls and I examined the case, the proprietress explained just how special these wands were. They were all handmade, with special powers attributed to each wand. She expounded on the spells and incantations that had been spoken and chanted by the wand-makers as they created these wands. They had been made by Druids, whose beliefs are rooted in some of the blackest, most evil witchcraft on this earth. She stated that each wand possessed magical power. However, she claimed that if they were used for evil, they would wither up and stop working.

So these were real wands that this store was selling. They were like Harry Potter wands on steroids. They were beautiful pieces of work, but they were nonetheless very evil. I have no doubt in my mind that if you were to purchase one and take it home, it would be like signing a contract with the devil to come into your life. I have seen it happen; objects can carry very powerful curses and spiritual junk.

This wasn't the only witchcraft store in London. This beautiful city has a large number of merchandisers who sell occult and New Age paraphernalia, catering to the growing industry of witchcraft and paganism. As I walked among the display cases and shelves, it hit me: how did the same country that had given us C.S. Lewis become steeped in Harry Potter?

Slippery Slope

England used to be a stronghold of the Christian faith; now those who identify themselves as Christian are in the minority, as paganism and popular witchcraft sects are making a comeback. How did a country that gave us the Magna Carta and a great religious heritage degenerate into a pagan society whose morals and beliefs are at an all-time low? England is a hotbed for witchcraft and satanic activity.

And England is where America is headed. We are a bit behind, but not by much. Throughout Western Europe, you can see the blueprint that the United States is likely to follow. After being in England and assessing the spiritual climate, it is disturbing to see similar trends developing in the United States. Standards of morality are becoming antiquated, and the Judeo-Christian faith is being superseded by agnosticism, if not outright atheism. Proponents of witchcraft and occult practices have begun a public relations campaign to put a nice and hip façade on their commonly looked-down-upon practices. Witchcraft has lost its fearsomeness and is being advertised as an alternative form of earth-loving spirituality.

As Savannah, Tess, and I interacted with and encountered the people of England, I was struck by a few common denominators exhibited among most of the people. Now of course there are remarkable exceptions and we were blessed to meet many faithful Brits who were on fire for the Lord. But in general, I noticed some discouraging trends in British society.

A general ignorance of all things spiritual is pervasive. While most Londoners may define themselves as "Christian," for many, their faith amounts to attending formal Easter and Christmas church services. Most people know the basics of many religions and beliefs, but their knowledge doesn't go past the surface. They do not see the point of worrying about such things, because they believe they are unaffected by them. Many people seem atheistic or agnostic in their beliefs, politely nodding their heads at the appropriate times, but walking away, shaking their heads at the Christians. The general attitude is that of simply not caring. The Church of England, staid and ritualistic as it is, makes it hard for people to grasp the reality of God and His power. Unless someone happens to be involved with supernatural things, the people live their lives as if the supernatural world doesn't exist. Many don't think it does.

Satan is taking full advantage of this ignorance.

Playing with Fire

One day the BBC took us to an old abbey to take some promo shots for the documentary. We were awed by the beautiful Waltham Abbey Church, which was completed in the year 1060 A.D., a century before Westminster Abbey was built. We had no idea what to expect, and as we walked around the grounds and church, we were struck by the beauty and rich history of the church. We have nothing to compare it to in America, and we really enjoyed exploring the interior of the historic church, as the BBC producers filmed us.

I was drawn to the front of the church, where there was a beautiful, elaborately decorated altar. While I was up front admiring the artwork, Tess and Savannah made an interesting discovery. Upon entering the church, their gaze had been pulled upward to the unique ceiling artwork. Interposed among the angels and paintings of biblical characters was a horoscope! Even in an old church, ancient occult practices had been able to worm their way in!

Another day, to promote the event we were having at a local church, our ministry team headed to Stratford station to hand out flyers. Stratford station is on the subway line and is one of the busier stops. The local church group that was hosting us was accustomed to doing this type of outreach, but for Tess, Savannah, and I, it was a first. To be truthful, I was a bit nervous. Here we were in a foreign country, talking about Jesus and handing out flyers to random strangers to invite them to come and see our deliverance seminar!...not to mention the added pressure of the ever-present BBC cameras, there to catch the action. We each took a stack and hit the pavement, handing out flyers right and left, answering questions for hours.

The young people were fascinated by what we had to say, and I think the mixture of the cameras and crosses combined and helped to pull them in. But while they showed a clear interest in who we were and what we were about, they had no knowledge of anything spiritual or godly. In fact, some teenagers had never before heard the gospel message. Isn't that sad? England used to be one of the most Christianized countries in the world. Now, the common teenager on the street has never even heard about God.

We met many interesting people during that time at Stratford Station. One young man in particular stands out in my memory. Sam was walking around the nearby mall with his buddies when they saw us handing out flyers. Curious, they came over and struck up a conversation with my dad. He noticed right away what Sam was wearing on a necklace around his neck—a pentagram with a goat interposed on it.

A pentagram is an occult symbol of satanic worship, and so is the goat, which is a symbol of Baphomet—one of the forms in which Lucifer appears. To wear one around your neck is no laughing matter. Yet Sam had no clue about the significance of what he was wearing. He was surprised to find out how evil his necklace really was. He had never really heard the gospel before, but was willing to let us pray over the necklace and more importantly him. He had a couple of his friends with him and they watched wide-eyed as my dad put his cross on Sam's forehead and prayed over any dark supernatural forces at work in Sam's life. It was so encouraging to see how open and interested Sam and his friends were in what we had to say. Sure, they might not have been very knowledgeable in spiritual matters, but they made up for it in openness and curiosity.

We talked with Sam a bit, and encouraged him to come to our meeting the next night. It was obvious that he was under heavy spiritual oppression, and we wanted to do more for him. The next day rolled around and Sam showed up at our meeting with his girlfriend. They watched in fascination as Dad preached a message and then we began to cast out demons. They looked shocked, and I can't say that I blame them! That was a lot to take in. I think more teenagers like Sam need to face the reality of evil and what evil is capable of.

Sam and his girlfriend watched as a sweet, churchgoing lady manifested violent demons, and they watched as the power of God drove out those demons. Most importantly, they got to experience the people of God as well as the presence of God in that small church. They had never seen anything like it, because Sam had never really been in a church before. I wish I could say stories like Sam's are the exception, but sadly, this is the cultural norm.

After the meeting, Sam looked a little freaked out. He was adamant about not having anything more to do with the occult after what he had seen. He had been given the opportunity to see what evil is really like, and he wanted no more part in it. Then he pulled out of the backpack a homemade Ouija Board. He had made it in school with his teacher. He was quite proud of it, and on a whim had brought it to our seminar that night.

An Ouija Board is used to contact demons and brings heavy spiritual oppression. After witnessing the exorcism and hearing what an Ouija Board really is, he wanted to destroy it then and there. So we prayed over the board as well as Sam and then had him break it. As he chucked the pieces in a trash can, he flashed a big smile and went on his way with his girlfriend. It was heartening to have met Sam and to have become part of his story. I pray that what he saw that night will never leave him.

The result of the spiritual ignorance and apathy that is so prevalent in England is that the occult, dark side of spirituality has sunk its hooks deeply into British soil. Now it has become a common occurrence to have your palm read, to check your daily horoscope, to have Harry-Potter-themed

Sunday schools, and to frequent witchcraft establishments. If you think there is no spiritual consequence to doing any of this, then why not partake in the "fun"? It is fascinating. If you are unaware of the dark supernatural forces at work, then it might seem like there cannot be any harm in indulging in some divination or sorcery. However, there is a very real cost to playing around with fire, and the heavy spiritual oppression in England is only beginning to be obvious.

As I noted, America had better beware. We are headed down the same path of apathy and moral ambiguity. Spiritual warfare is becoming more of a fairy tale and less of a reality in this world. However as Christians, we know that, "we do not wrestle against flesh and blood, but against principalities, against powers, against the rulers of the darkness of this age, against spiritual hosts of wickedness in the heavenly places" (Ephesians 6:12). We can reverse this descent into spiritual darkness. We can stop the moral decay in America. It will be an uphill battle, we have already given so much ground, but it is possible. Don't let America become the new Britain, sold out to the dark side of the supernatural.

CHAPTER 10

Love in a Millennial Generation

> About three things I was absolutely positive. First, Edward was a vampire. Second, there was a part of him—and I didn't know how potent that part might be—that thirsted for my blood. And third, I was unconditionally and irrevocably in love with him.
>
> —Stephanie Meyer, *Twilight*

I am a part of a new generation. This generation is unique. We will face things that our parents never faced, in a world that is becoming scarier and more dangerous. We will be challenged in ways that our ancestors could not have imagined. We are the "millennials." Born in the 1990s, this college-age population has been the subject of many studies and stories. We are growing up in a drastically changing world. The United States is drifting away from the morals and beliefs that once made her great. Once strongly Judeo-Christian, the proud symbol of freedom, moral decay now eats away at America's foundations while poor leadership and a teetering economy threaten the stability of the nation. Abroad, other countries are becoming bolder in their disgust for America. There is no peace. This is the land that my peers and I will inherit.

One of the biggest changes that has affected the minds of millennials is the changing moral fabric of society. With admirable stealth, atheism and humanism have crept into our schoolrooms and even our churches. Shockingly, about 70 percent of young adults leave the church once they enter their twenties. Moral absolutes are passé; right and wrong are relative. The mottoes are, "Do what feels good," and "look out for Number One." Unrecognized sin leaves a person of any age wide open to severe spiritual oppression.

Love Under Siege

Love is under attack. The evil one is distorting and perverting our perception of love: how we love others, especially romance, as well as our relationship with the One who loves unconditionally, the Lord Himself. Why would Satan target love and romance? Because Satan is the antithesis of love. He is hate. He despises love, which is one of the most powerful things in the world.

It's true: "God is love" (1 John 4:8, 16). He saved all who would believe in Him by sending His Son Jesus to die on a cross: "For God so loved the world that He gave His only begotten Son, that whoever believes in Him should not perish but have everlasting life" (John 3:16). You and I have been saved from death because of *love*. Love defeated Satan on the cross, and he hates it.

In addition to that, love is also the greatest commandment. A man came to Jesus and asked Him which of all the laws was the greatest. Jesus answered,

> *"You shall love the Lord your God with all your heart, with all your soul, and with all your mind."* This is the first and great commandment. And the second is like it: *"You shall love your neighbor as yourself."* On these two commandments hang all the Law and the Prophets. (Matthew 22:37–40)

No wonder the devil has tried so hard to pervert love.

What is love? We all know what love is, but when asked to define it, many stammer. Yet all people from every religious background (or no religion at all) recognize that love is extremely powerful. All human beings long to be loved. This is because we were *made* to love and be loved.

Love is not merely a Christian ideal; love spans all ages, religions, and cultures. People from all walks of life recognize the authority of love. Mahatma Gandhi, Indian Hindu leader and a promoter of non-violent resistance wrote that, "Where there is love, there is life." Famous English novelist and playwright John Galsworthy accurately pointed out that, "Love has no age, no limit; and no death." Israeli Prime Minister Benjamin Disraeli contended that, "We are all born for love. It is the principle of existence, and its only end." One atheist explains love as, "Serving an important biological function. Humans developed the ability to experience feelings of love because it helps keep social groups and families together, and bonds parents and children."

OK, so love is pretty important to everyone. In the modern world, "love" has been redefined and contorted until it is unrecognizable, featured as the key force in racy romance novels, "adult" movies, and all forms of pornography, including pedophilia, incubus/succubus, and bestiality. Even as recently as fifty years ago, most of these expressions of "love" were kept under wraps. But now every teenager and young adult is assaulted with a constant stream of sexual and graphic images. Just walk up the teen/young adult aisle in your local bookstore. The trash on display will certainly take you aback. They promote love gone wrong.

HOOKING UP. We live in a hook-up culture. Casual sex and sex outside of marriage has become the norm. No longer do people wait to get married before becoming intimate, and this has almost become expected in society. By age fifteen, 16 percent of teens have had a sexual experience; by age sixteen, it's up to 33 percent. Nearly half (48 percent) of those seventeen-year-olds are no longer virgins, and on up: 61 percent of eighteen-year-olds and 71 percent of nineteen-year-olds (according to the Guttmacher Institute's May 2014 Fact Sheet). I am attending a Christian university, and I was honestly surprised at how many students there have hooked up with someone or slept around. It seems as if most everyone's story involves premarital sex, and it never seems to end well. Since I am in a ministry leadership position at my school, I've spent a lot of time talking with girls and hearing their stories. My heart breaks to hear the pain these young women have been through at such a young age. And to think that most of the pain they have suffered could have been avoided.

Here are the dangers that I see in engaging in premarital sex:

It violates God's moral law. Many have not even heard that sex before marriage is not how God intended it to be. In the Bible, God has given specific commands to His people to abstain from sexual immorality. Hebrews 13:4, for example, charges, "Let marriage be held in honor among all, and let the marriage bed be undefiled, for God will judge the sexually immoral and adulterous" (NASB). Sleeping with someone just because you love him or her is not a good enough reason. God placed sex within the bounds of marriage for some very important reasons. It is for our own good that we abstain from sexual immorality.

The two shall become one flesh. Early on in his ministry, my father discovered, to his surprise, that when he ministered to married couples, they had the same demonic issues! When he worked with people who had slept around, they seemed to have picked up their partner's demons. Sometimes even men and women who had been sexually abused shared their abuser's spiritual bondage. How is this possible? Can people catch each other's spiritual oppression? In a way, yes. When two people get married, they "cleave unto each other." (The word cleave means to glue together.) A part of this cleaving is when the two share a marriage bed. When people have sex, they become *one flesh*. Jesus, quoting Genesis 1:27, 5:2, and 2:24, spoke about this directly: "from the beginning of the creation, God 'made them male and female.' 'For this reason a man shall leave his father and mother and be joined to his wife, and the two shall become one flesh'; so then they are no longer two, but one flesh" (Mark 10:6–8).

With the physical union comes a spiritual union. Within the bounds of a healthy marriage, this is a good thing. But spiritual junk can pass from one person to another. I have seen it again and again; it's one of the devil's favorite tricks: STDs (sexually transmitted demons). From an exorcist's perspective, not only can sleeping around get you into spiritual bondage because you are breaking God's moral law, but you can also pick up evil spirits along the way! Sex binds two people together emotionally, physically, and spiritually. If the devil can exploit that, he will.

LIVING TOGETHER. Recently, as I was scrolling my Facebook feed, something caught my eye. It was a post by a friend of mine, who is a Christian. Here is what caught my eye: "Why I think it's OK to live with your boyfriend." She then tried to justify why she believed it was OK to live together as a couple without being married. Sadly, this is the viewpoint of many.

A study done in 2013 revealed that, by the age of thirty, three-quarters of unmarried American women have lived with a partner. Researchers believe that cohabitation is becoming a regular part of family life in the United States, even though some studies seem to show that living together before marriage increases the chances of divorce, especially in a first marriage.

So, just because something is the norm or average does not mean it is OK. Unmarried people acting and living like they are married is not what God intended. Children need their parents to be in a fully committed relationship, having entered into a binding contract between man, wife, and God.

LOVE HOLLYWOOD-STYLE. The moral example being set by celebrities such as Beyonce and Katy Perry and others who are looked up to by teenage girls has fallen to an all-new low. It has almost become stylish to have children out of wedlock and to give them odd names and raise them in the spotlight. Why should we admire these people? Stars often have more dysfunctional and demon-filled lives than anyone else.

When singer Rihanna stayed with her boyfriend, Chris Brown, after a brutal beating that went public, think about the example that was set for young girls. What kind of message does their twisted relationship say about love and romance, especially to teens who are searching for role models? These stars that we have put on pedestals to emulate are setting horrible examples of how marriage is supposed to work. With all of the weekly on-again, off-again dramas over who is dating whom, is it any wonder that teens have a skewed conception about what true love is? The love and romance portrayed in popular songs, on the big screens, and on the red carpet is just a farce. Real love isn't supposed to be like that.

HUMANISTIC AND ATHEISTIC LOVE. While atheists will admit that love is very important, their argument is that emotions and loving actions simply evolved because we need them. They serve an important biological need and that's all. So of course there is no pure or perfect love. It is just an animalistic instinct to insure that our genes get passed down to the next generation. Loving relationships are seen only as highly developed survival strategies. To an atheist who believes that people do not have souls, love is merely electricity firing in the brain and there can be no soul-to-soul connection. The value of love is greatly cheapened, and there is no security or safety in love. Following this logic, love disappears as soon as the survival of the fittest kicks in.

However, true love doesn't match this view. Real love is self-sacrificing and puts others before itself. True love means being vulnerable and it is very risky; in fact the "fittest" may not survive as long as others, although they will not mind the sacrifice.

PRETERNATURAL LOVE. The quote at the beginning of this chapter perfectly sums up our fascination with preternatural (supernatural) love. We know it carries danger, but also passion. And its secretiveness and uniqueness have an unquestionable appeal. Vampire love, werewolf love, and even spiritual love (such as incubus and succubus) beckon many. Books have titles like *The Alpha's Quest* (a story of a woman and werewolf falling in love) or *The Demon of Darkling Reach*. This is fantasy love. It doesn't exist and it leads readers into dangerous spiritual territory. This kind of love has nothing to do with the Lord.

That being said, I do understand the appeal. In preparation for writing this book, I read the *Twilight* series. I did so carefully and from a research perspective, yet I'll admit the books drew me in. I couldn't put them down. There is something very raw and magnetic about the idea of a supernatural romance, the classic story of a girl who suddenly has the attention and love of a supernatural being. "He is amazing and could be with anyone, and he chose me!" Sadly, very few fans of this kind of fiction realize that the only supernatural being who can fill that need is God Himself.

FIFTY SHADES OF GREY LOVE. The popular book series, *Fifty Shades of Grey* is nothing more than a violent and perverted "romance" story with sadistic elements. Commonly referred to as "mommy porn," this type of book is steadily becoming more popular with all ages. *Fifty Shades of Grey* and other books of its ilk foster an absorption in romance novels and living in an adulterous or immoral world of the mind through steamy tales of coupling. Lustful romance novels like this set an unrealistic and fantastical perspective about love in readers' minds. How easily love has been cheapened and reduced to a cheap romance thrill. This kind of "love" isn't real love at all.

The Reality of Romance: God's Take on Love

Some will say that love can't be defined, that it has a different meaning to everyone. This is a cop-out to avoid the reality of what—and Who—love really is. The best definition of true love is from the Word of God, contained in the famous "love chapter" that the apostle Paul wrote to the Corinthian church.

Though I speak with the tongues of men and of angels, but have not love, I have become sounding brass or a clanging cymbal. And though I have the gift of prophecy, and understand all mysteries and all knowledge, and though I have all faith, so that I could remove mountains, but have not love, I am nothing. And though I bestow all my goods to feed the poor, and though I give my body to be burned, but have not love, it profits me nothing.

Love suffers long and is kind; love does not envy; love does not parade itself, is not puffed up; does not behave rudely, does not seek its own, is not provoked, thinks no evil; does not rejoice in iniquity, but rejoices in the truth; bears all things, believes all things, hopes all things, endures all things.

Love never fails. But whether there are prophecies, they will fail; whether there are tongues, they will cease; whether there is knowledge, it will vanish away. For we know in part and we prophesy in part. But when that which is perfect has come, then that which is in part will be done away.

When I was a child, I spoke as a child, I understood as a child, I thought as a child; but when I became a man,

I put away childish things. For now we see in a mirror, dimly, but then face to face. Now I know in part, but then I shall know just as I also am known.

And now abide faith, hope, love, these three; but the greatest of these is love. (1 Corinthians 13, emphasis mine)

This is perfect love, and we all fall short of such a high goal. The only one who is capable of perfect love is the One who created it, God Himself. He loves us with a perfect love, and all He invites us to do is love Him back with all of our heart, soul, and mind. We can be safe and secure in His love; He will never leave us or forsake us. Love has saved us and continues to fight for us.

Satan wants to disrupt and destroy our understanding of love and how we relate to each other and God. Love overcomes barriers between people, and Satan wants to separate us from each other.

Love is one of the most effective tools in ministering deliverance. Often I will be working with someone and facing off supernatural, evil forces when it hits me: *This person just needs love.* So I will lean over and just give them a hug, loving the person with the love of Christ. More often than not, breakthroughs happen when people feel that they are loved and cared for.

Experience That Love

Many people come from broken homes, or they have been used and abused by the people they care about most. Many have built so many walls and barriers around their hearts that they wonder if they still have one. One of life's harsh truths is that people will fail you. No one is perfect, and we all sin and let the ones we love down. In the world, to be open to love is to be open to pain.

But those harsh life lessons do not apply to our relationship with God. He is perfect love, and He will never let you down. With an everlasting love, God loves each individual who has ever lived or whoever will live. He doesn't change His mind about love and He doesn't change His heart. Hebrews 13:8 tells us that "Jesus Christ is the same yesterday, today, and forever." Because He is unchanging and perfect, He is capable of giving us a love that never disappoints! He can transform the most messed-up life into a life of true love.

The best part about it is that it is available to one and all! Anyone can come to Him, at any time. You and I can be safe and secure in His love, and we can know that no matter what we do, He will never stop loving us. Whether you are a Christian who has stagnated in your faith or someone who hasn't accepted the Lord yet, He still loves you.

God created us for love and he wants to give us that love. James 4:8 tells us to "Draw near to God and He will draw near to you." If you take that first step to draw near to the One who knows you and loves you because He made you, you will never regret it. You can trust Him with everything, and He will never let you down. Ask the Lord into your life. All you have to do is confess out loud that He is Lord, confess that you are a sinner, and believe in your heart that He is your God and Savior. Once you do that, He will come into your heart. And one day, you will be able to be with Him in heaven. No one needs to be "good enough" to come to Him. Romans 3:23 tells us that all have sinned and fallen short of the glory of God. Every single man, woman, and child is a sinner and in need of a Savior.

Open yourself up to God's love, let Him satisfy your craving for love—and thwart Satan's plan for your life! This is real love. It is so rich and fulfilling that once you have had a taste, you can't get enough. It is a love powerful enough to carry every single one of your sins away. Jesus died a horrendous death on the cross to cancel out those sins. He paid for them with His blood. Now you and I are liberated to come into God's presence, and this is what we were made for, to love and be loved by God.

The devil tries to pervert the truth until the end of the world, and sadly, he will catch many in his snares, but that doesn't have to include you. What will you fill the

God-shaped hole in your heart with? Fill it with the real thing, with God's love. Don't give a second glance to the dark side of the supernatural, with its facsimile of love and false peace.

As 1 Peter 5:8–9 says, "Be sober, be vigilant; because your adversary the devil walks about like a roaring lion, seeking whom he may devour. Resist him, steadfast in the faith."